play guitar with...
classic metal

Your Guarantee of Quality
*As publishers, we strive to produce every book
to the highest commercial standards.
The music has been freshly engraved and the book has
been carefully designed to minimise awkward page turns
and to make playing from it a real pleasure.
Particular care has been given to specifying acid-free,
neutral-sized paper made from pulps which have not been
elemental chlorine bleached. This pulp is from farmed
sustainable forests and was produced with special regard
for the environment.
Throughout, the printing and binding have been planned
to ensure a sturdy, attractive publication which should
give years of enjoyment.
If your copy fails to meet our high standards,
please inform us and we will gladly replace it.*

play guitar with...
classic metal

HAL LEONARD EUROPE
Distributed by Music Sales Limited

Published by
Hal Leonard Europe
A Music Sales/Hal Leonard Joint Venture Company
14-15 Berners Street, London W1T 3LJ, UK.

Exclusive Distributors:
MUSIC SALES LIMITED
Distribution Centre, Newmarket Road,
Bury St Edmunds, Suffolk IP33 3YB, UK.

Order No. HLE90004464
ISBN 978-1-78038-379-8
This book © Copyright 2012 Hal Leonard Europe.

Unauthorised reproduction of any part of this publication by any means including photocopying is an infringement of copyright.

Printed in the EU

www.musicsales.com

Edited by Adrian Hopkins
Cover designed by Liz Barrand

Ace Of Spades;
Breaking The Law;
The Boys Are Back In Town;
Paranoid:
Guitars: Arthur Dick
Bass: Paul Townsend
Drums: Noam Lederman

The Number Of the Beast:
Guitars: Arthur Dick
Bass: Paul Townsend
Drums: Brett Morgan

Recorded and mixed by Jonas Persson

Smoke On the Water &
Pour Some Sugar On Me:
Tracking, mixing, and mastering by
Jake Johnson & Bill Maynard at Paradyme Productions
Guitars by Doug Boduch
Bass by Tom McGirr
Keyboards by Warren Wiegratz
Drums by Scott Schroedl

- 10 **ace of spades** motörhead
- thin lizzy the boys are back in town 16
- judas priest **breaking the law** 25
- 30 the number of the beast iron maiden
- black sabbath **paranoid** 46
- 52 pour some sugar on me def leppard
- deep purple **smoke on the water** 41

guitar tablature explained

Guitar music can be explained in three different ways: on a musical stave, in tablature, and in rhythm slashes.

RHYTHM SLASHES: are written above the stave. Strum chords in the rhythm indicated. Round noteheads indicate single notes.

THE MUSICAL STAVE: shows pitches and rhythms and is divided by lines into bars. Pitches are named after the first seven letters of the alphabet.

TABLATURE: graphically represents the guitar fingerboard. Each horizontal line represents a string, and each number represents a fret.

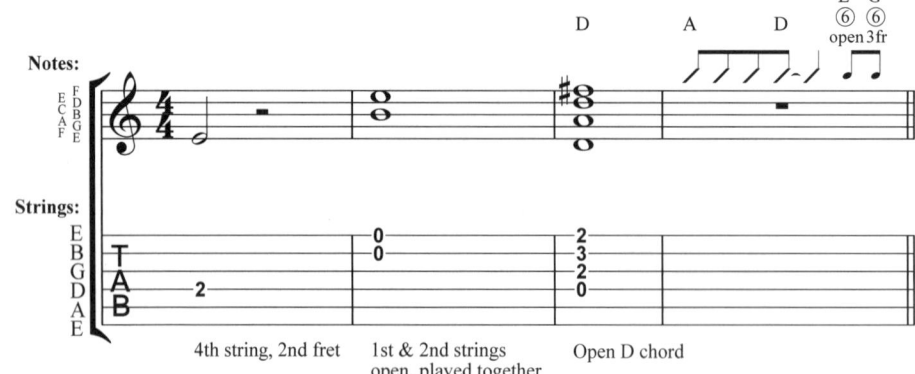

definitions for special guitar notation

SEMI-TONE BEND: Strike the note and bend up a semi-tone (½ step).

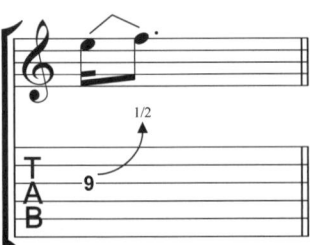

WHOLE-TONE BEND: Strike the note and bend up a whole-tone (full step).

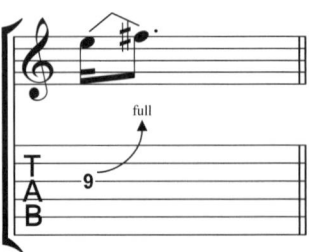

GRACE NOTE BEND: Strike the note and bend as indicated. Play the first note as quickly as possible.

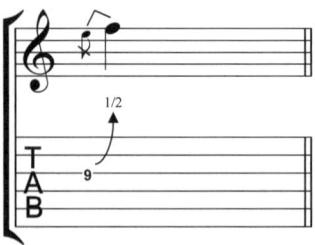

QUARTER-TONE BEND: Strike the note and bend up a ¼ step

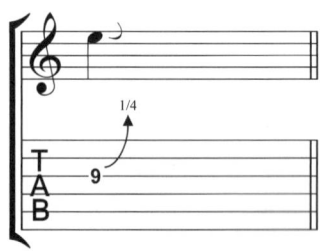

BEND & RELEASE: Strike the note and bend up as indicated, then release back to the original note.

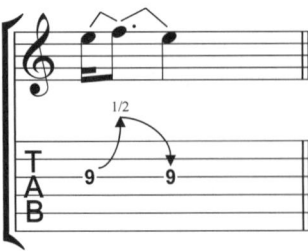

COMPOUND BEND & RELEASE: Strike the note and bend up and down in the rhythm indicated.

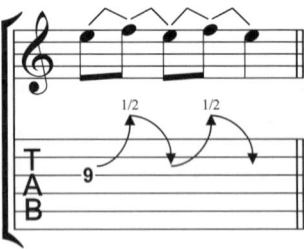

PRE-BEND: Bend the note as indicated, then strike it.

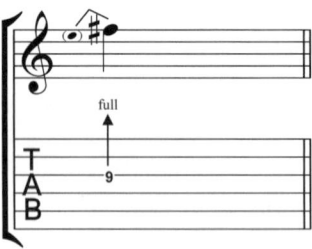

PRE-BEND & RELEASE: Bend the note as indicated. Strike it and release the note back to the original pitch.

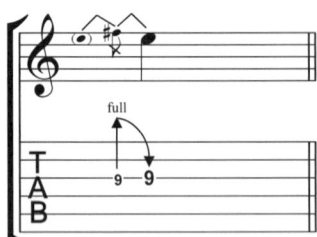

HAMMER-ON: Strike the first note with one finger, then sound the second note (on the same string) with another finger by fretting it without picking.

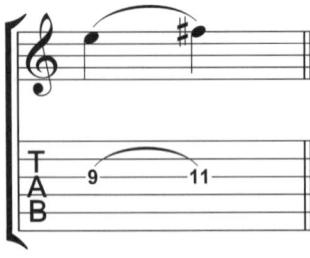

PULL-OFF: Place both fingers on the note to be sounded, strike the first note and without picking, pull the finger off to sound the second note.

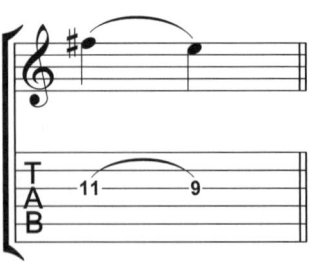

LEGATO SLIDE (GLISS): Strike the first note and then slide the same fret-hand finger up or down to the second note. The second note is not struck.

MUFFLED STRINGS: A percussive sound is produced by laying the first hand across the string(s) without depressing, and striking them with the pick hand.

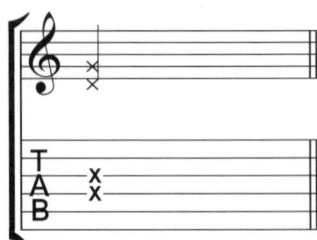

NATURAL HARMONIC: Strike the note while the fret-hand lightly touches the string directly over the fret indicated.

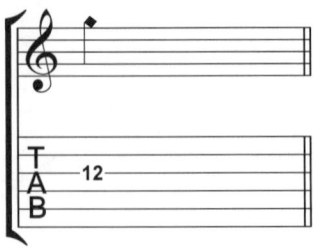

PICK SCRAPE: The edge of the pick is rubbed down (or up) the string, producing a scratchy sound.

PALM MUTING: The note is partially muted by the pick hand lightly touching the string(s) just before the bridge.

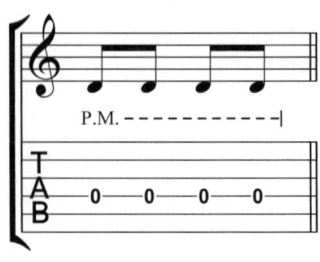

SHIFT SLIDE (GLISS & RESTRIKE) Same as legato slide, except the second note is struck.

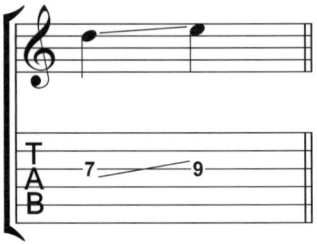

TAP HARMONIC: The note is fretted normally and a harmonic is produced by tapping or slapping the fret indicated in brackets (which will be twelve frets higher than the fretted note.)

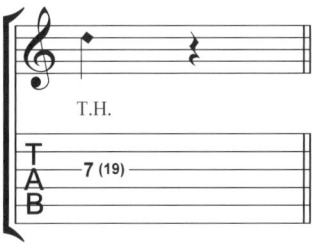

TAPPING: Hammer ('tap') the fret indicated with the pick-hand index or middle finger and pull-off to the note fretted by the fret hand.

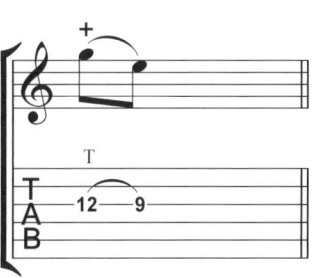

PINCH HARMONIC: The note is fretted normally and a harmonic is produced by adding the edge of the thumb or the tip of the index finger of the pick hand to the normal pick attack.

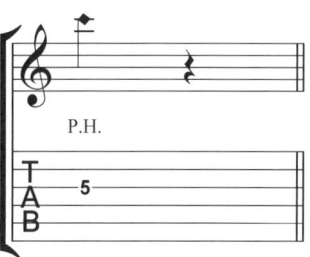

ARTIFICIAL HARMONIC: The note fretted normally and a harmonic is produced by gently resting the pick hand's index finger directly above the indicated fret (in brackets) while plucking the appropriate string.

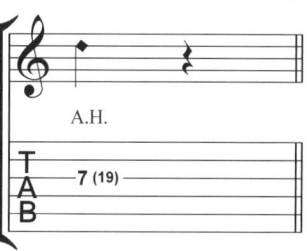

TRILL: Very rapidly alternate between the notes indicated by continuously hammering-on and pulling-off.

RAKE: Drag the pick across the strings with a single motion.

TREMOLO PICKING: The note is picked as rapidly and continuously as possible.

ARPEGGIATE: Play the notes of the chord indicated by quickly rolling them from bottom to top.

SWEEP PICKING: Rhythmic downstroke and/or upstroke motion across the strings.

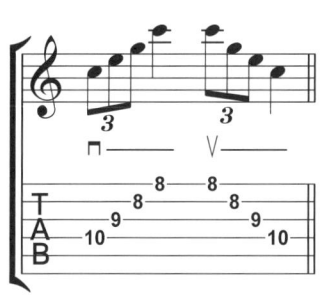

VIBRATO DIVE BAR AND RETURN: The pitch of the note or chord is dropped a specific number of steps (in rhythm) then returned to the original pitch.

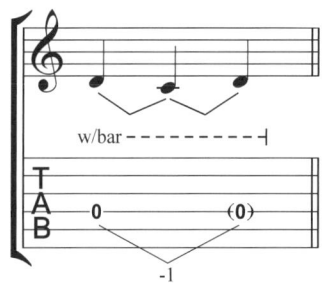

VIBRATO BAR SCOOP: Depress the bar just before striking the note, then quickly release the bar.

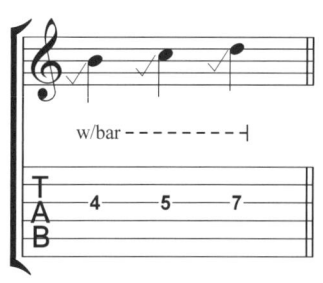

VIBRATO BAR DIP: Strike the note and then immediately drop a specific number of steps, then release back to the original pitch.

additional musical definitions

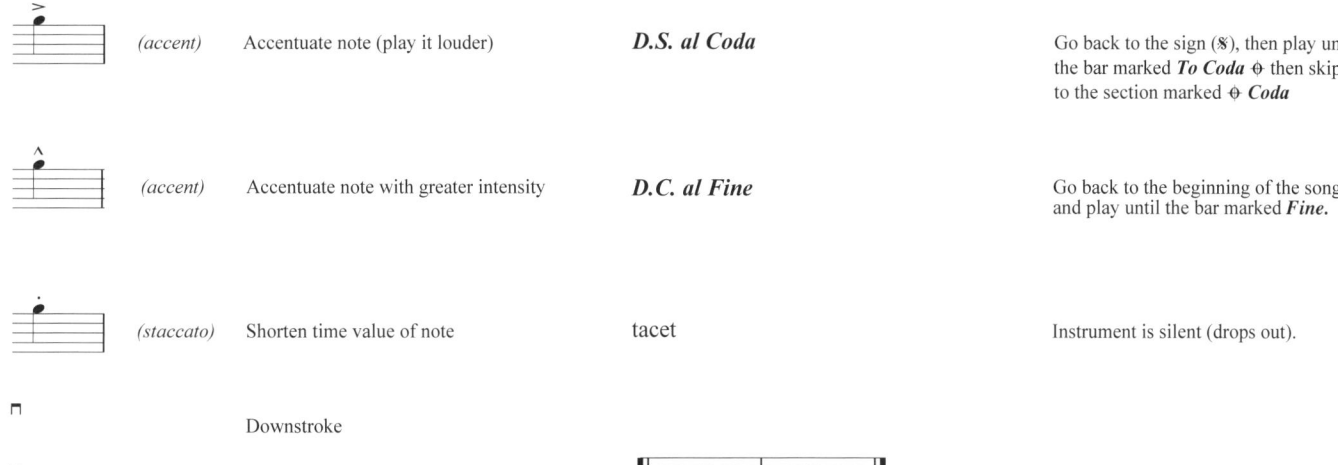

NOTE: Tablature numbers in brackets mean:
1. The note is sustained, but a new articulation (such as hammer-on or slide) begins
2. A note may be fretted but not necessarily played.

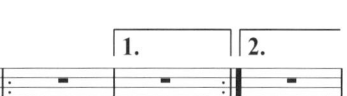

When a repeat section has different endings, play the first ending only the first time and the second ending only the second time.

ace of spades

**Words and Music by
Ian Kilmister, Eddie Clarke & Phil Taylor**

© Copyright 1980 Motor Music Limited.
All Rights Reserved. International Copyright Secured.

Full performance demo: track 1
Backing only: track 8

To match recording, tune down a semitone
Intro
1 bar count in:

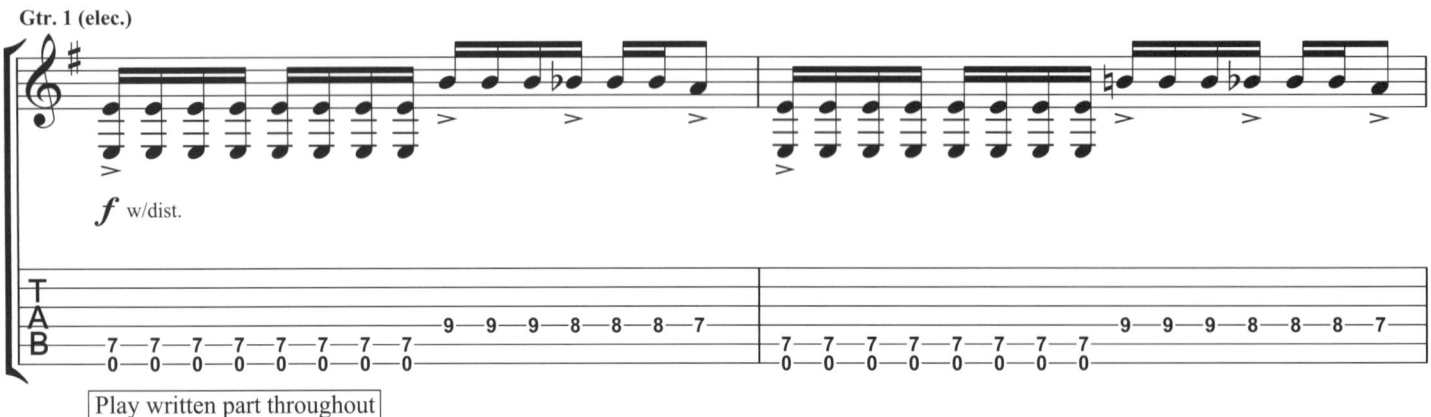

Play written part throughout

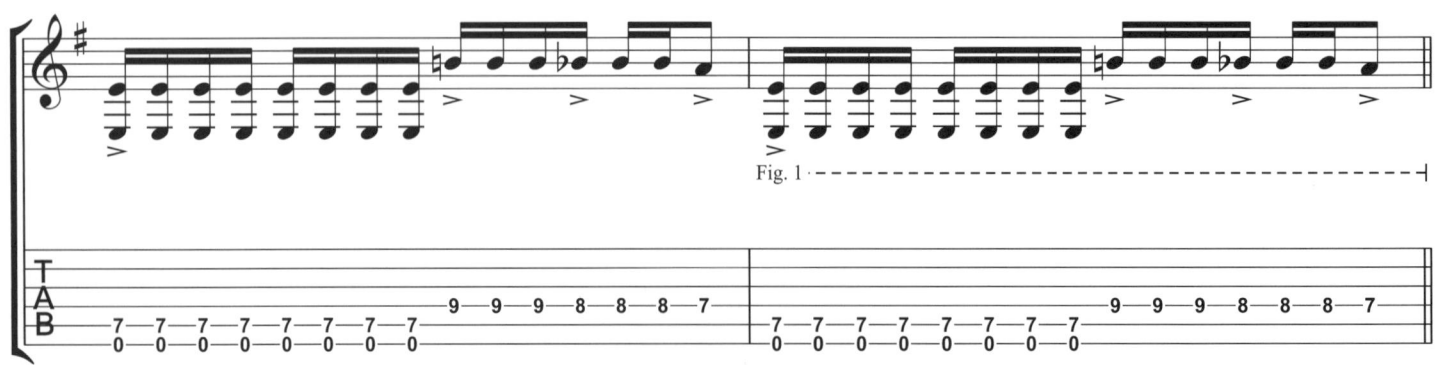

10

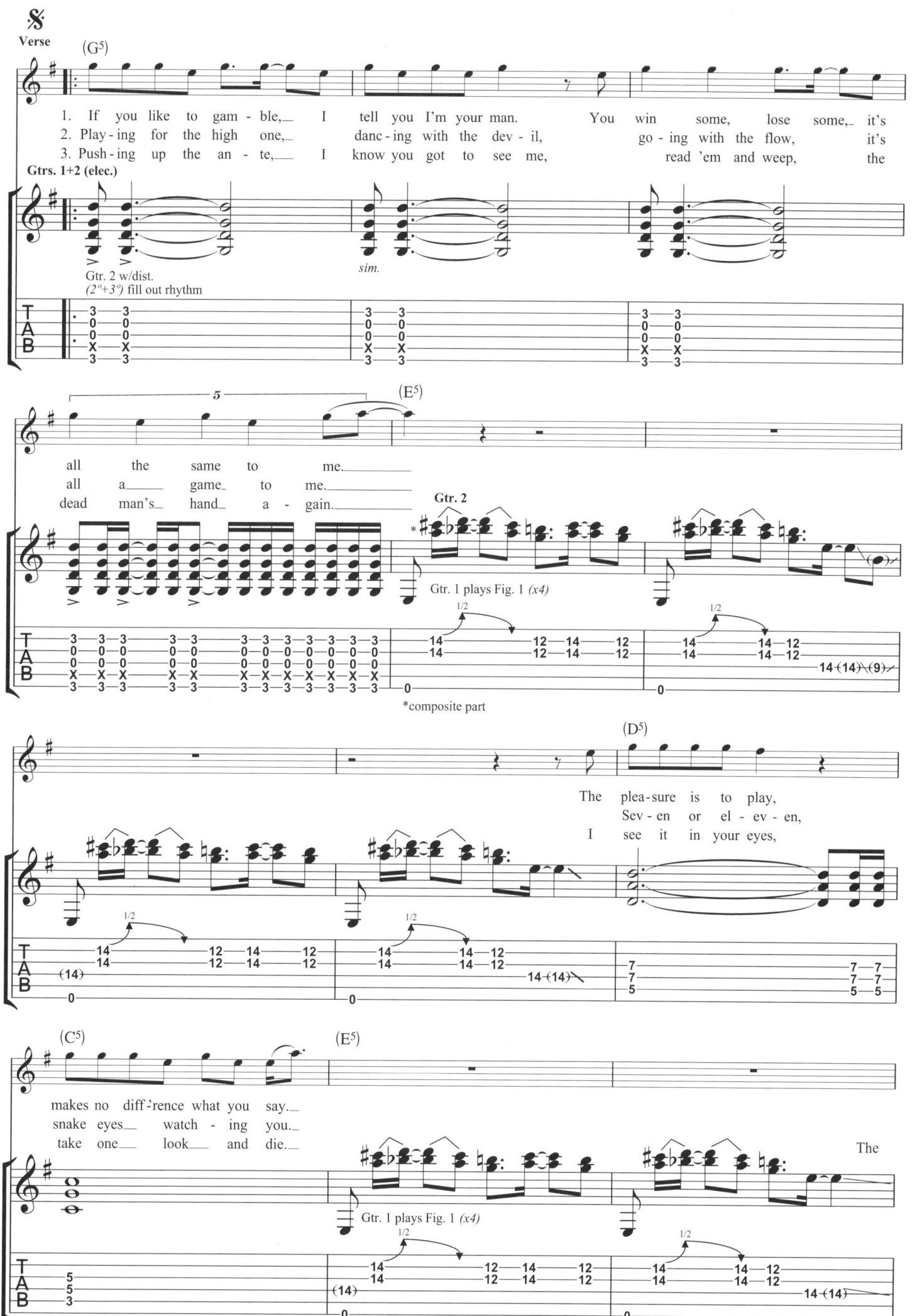

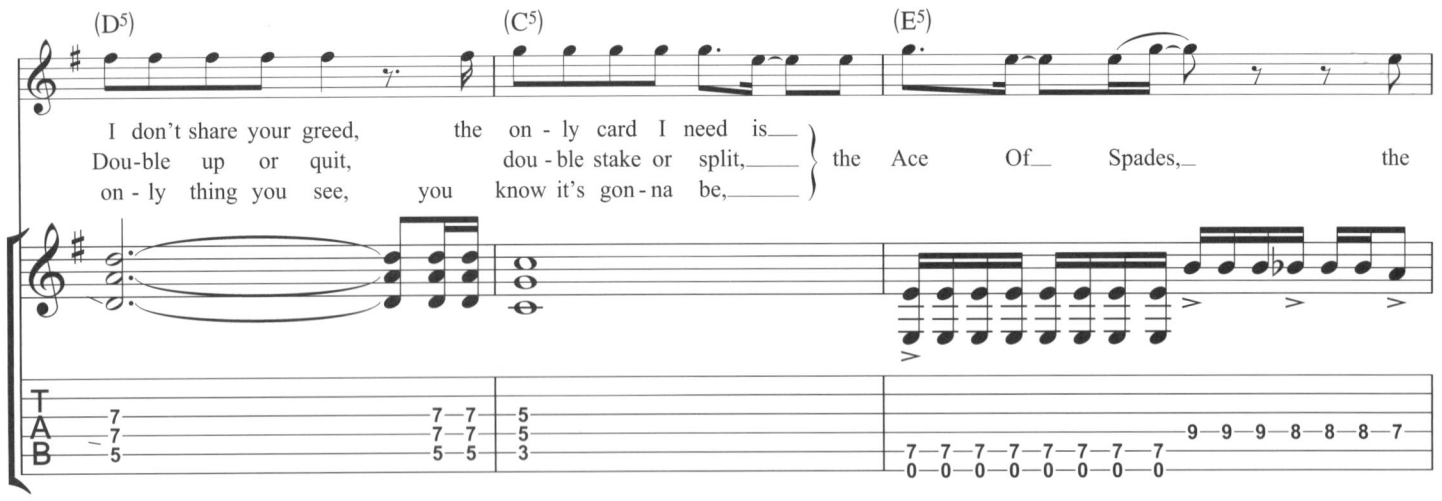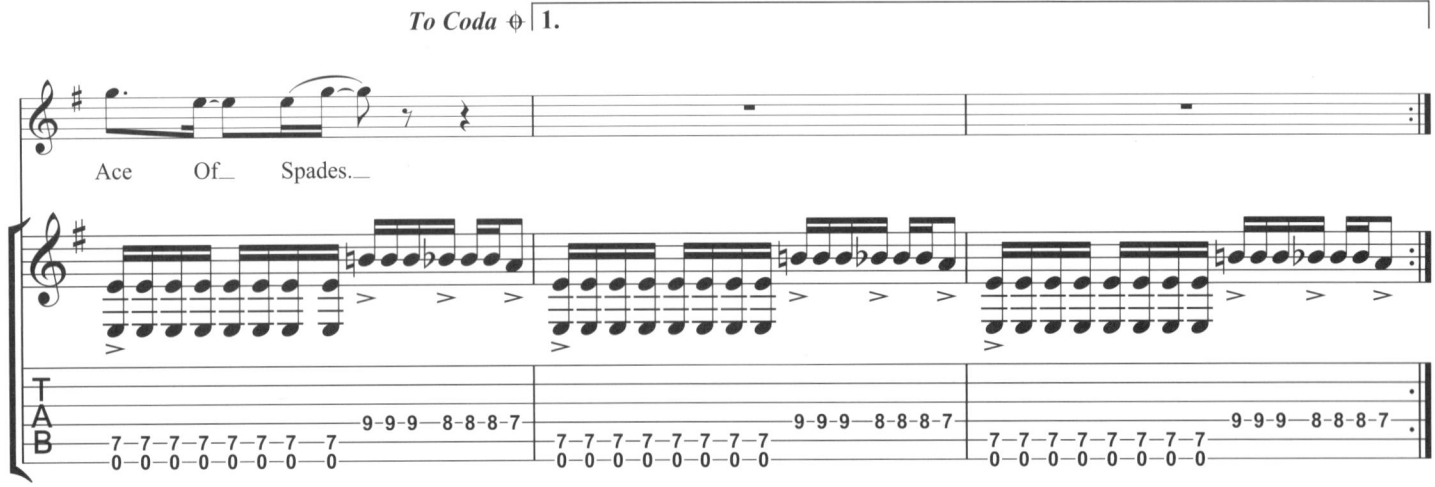

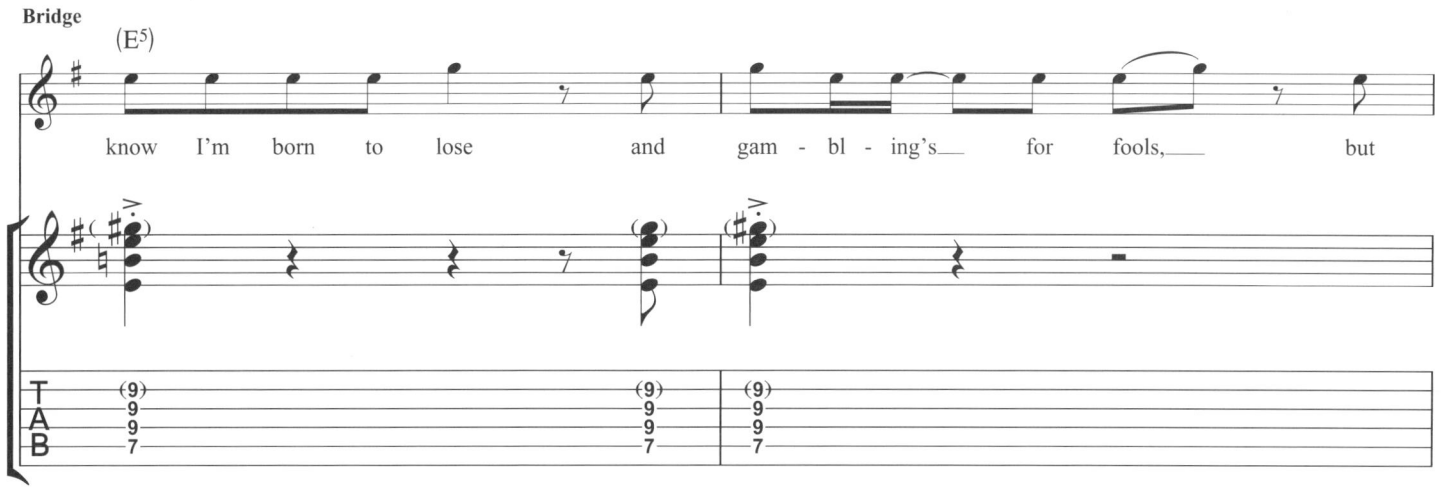

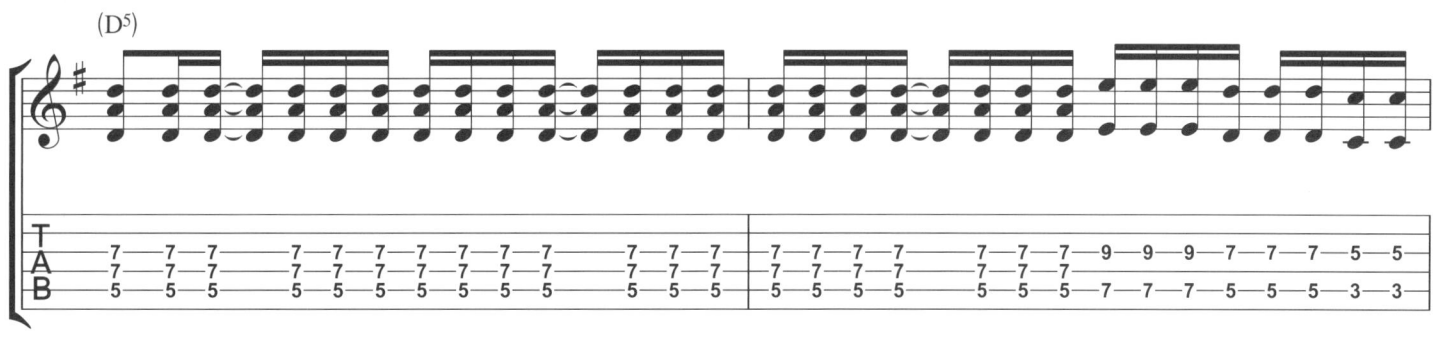

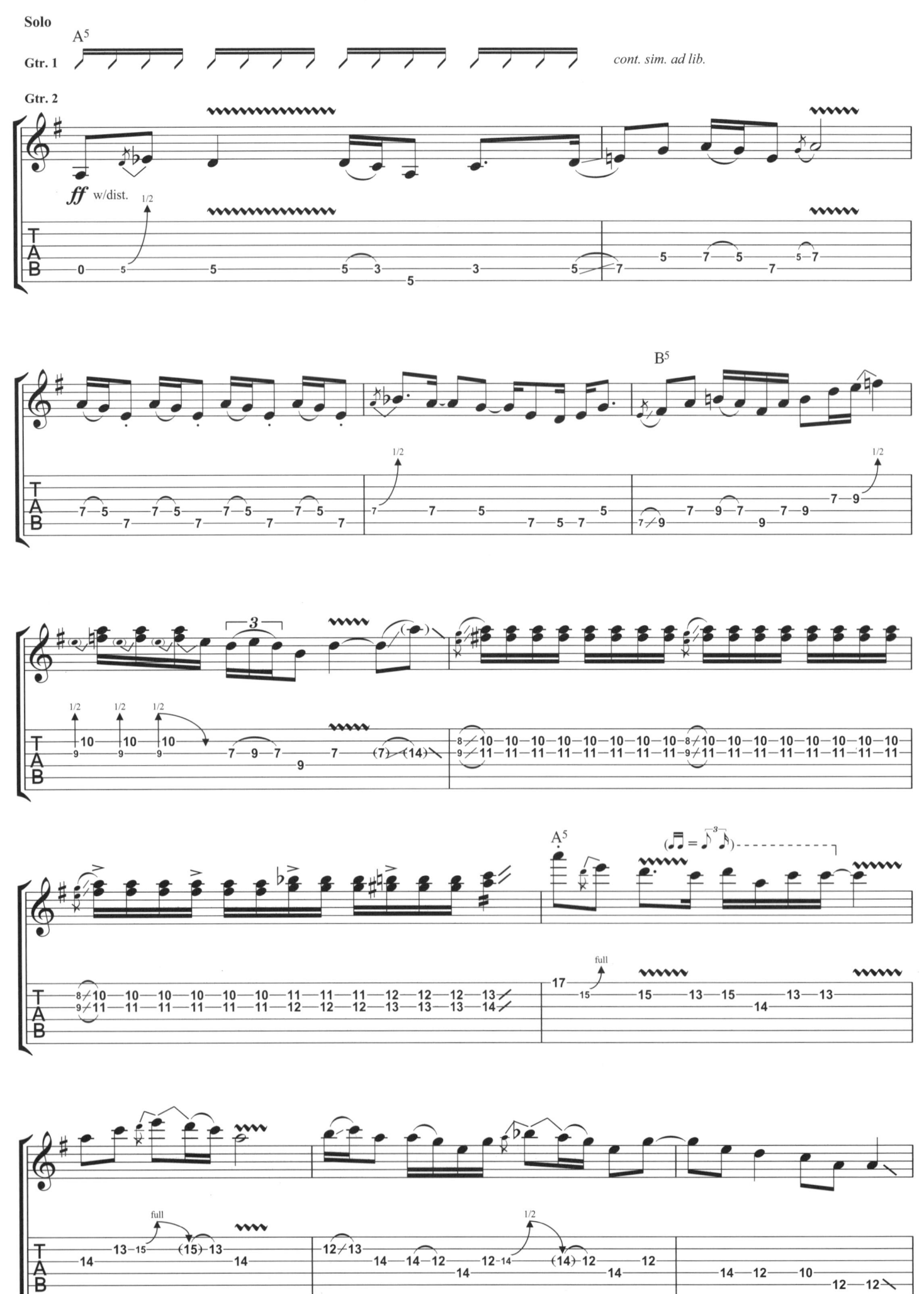

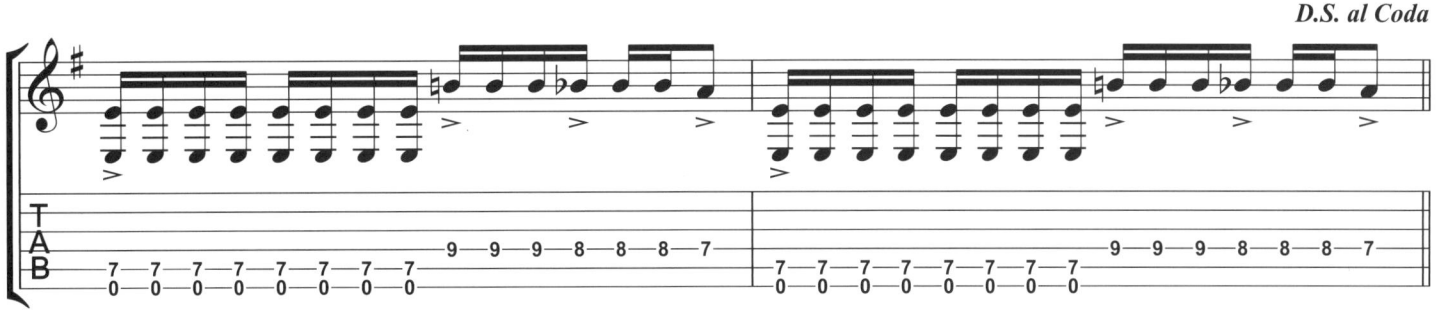
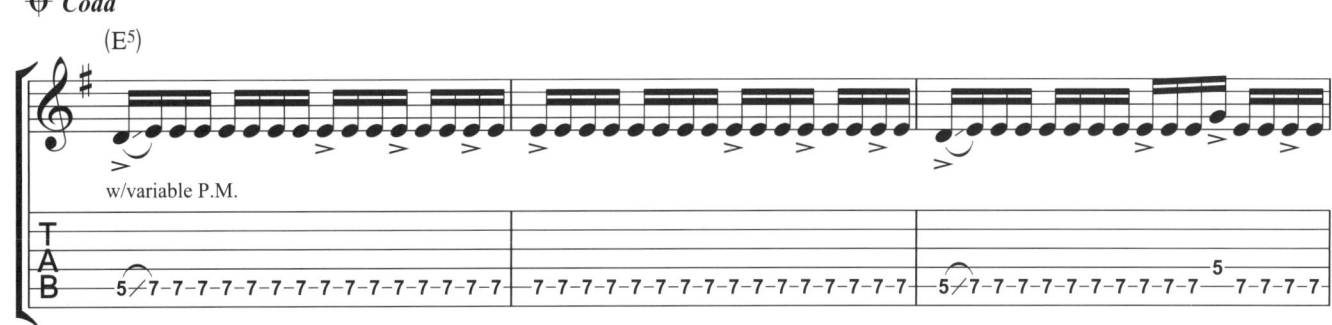
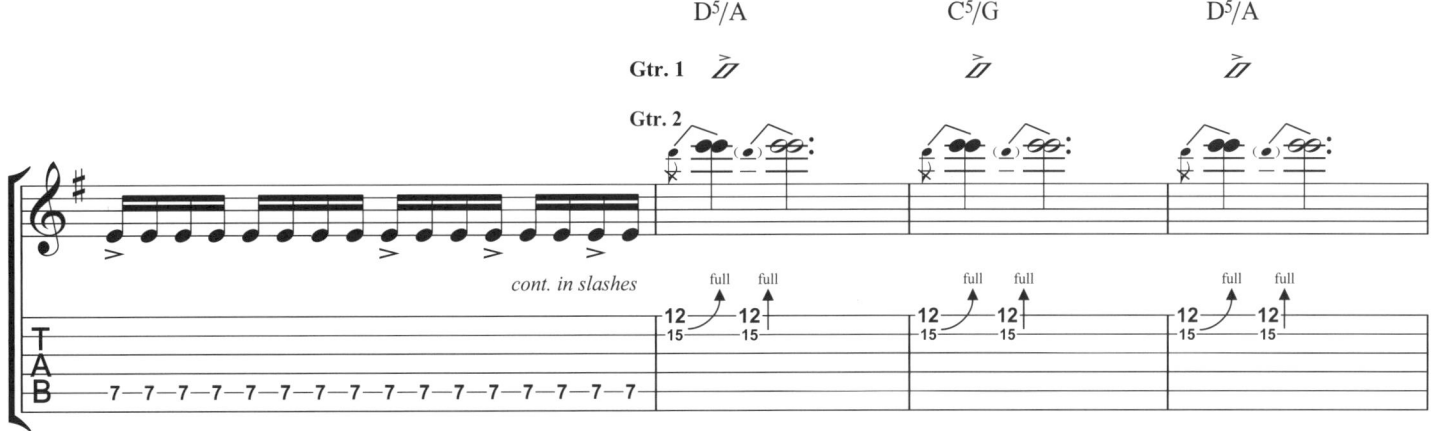

the boys are back in town

**Words and Music by
Phil Lynott**

© Copyright 1976 Pippin The Friendly Ranger Music Company Limited.
Universal Music Publishing Limited.
All rights in Germany administered by Universal Music Publ. GmbH.
All Rights Reserved. International Copyright Secured.

Full performance demo: track 2
Backing only: track 9

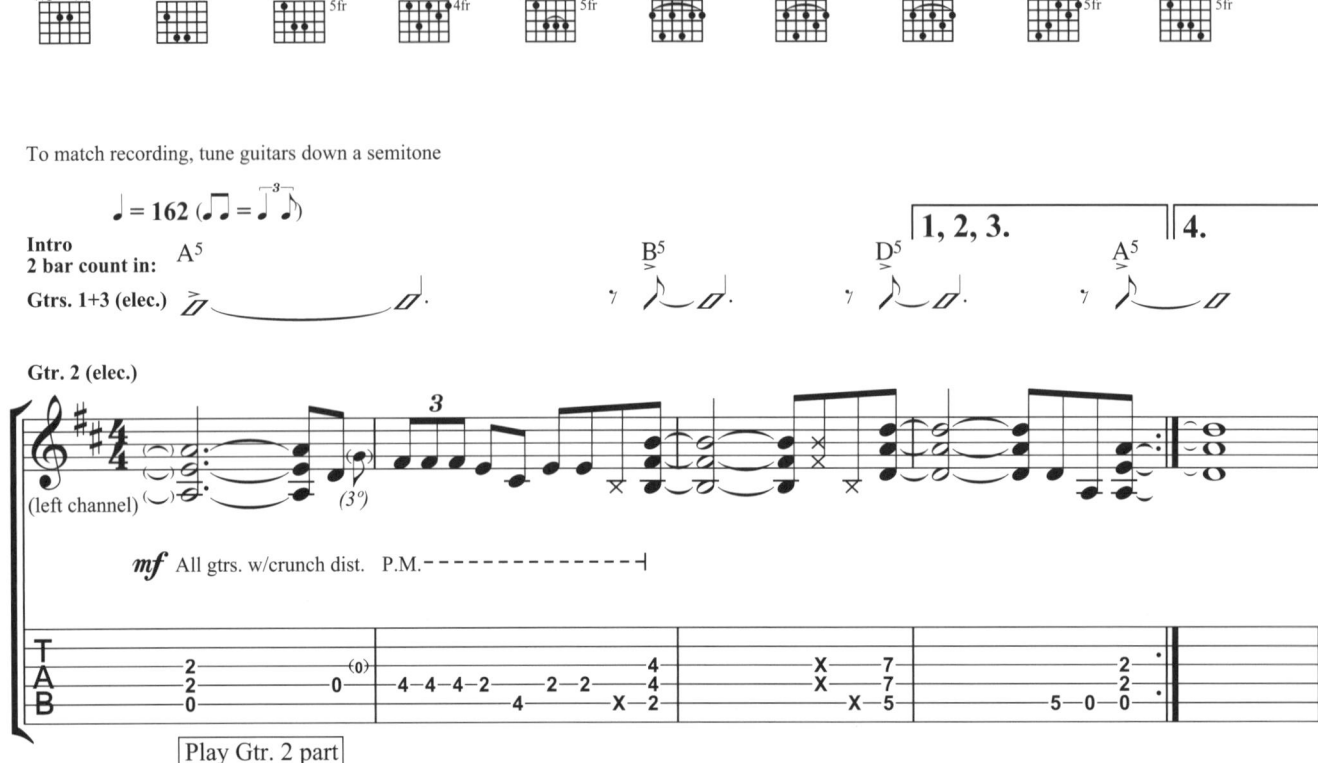

16

F♯7sus4
Bm7
Bm7/E
Have - n't changed, had - n't much to say, but man, I still think them
Man, when I tell you she was cool, she was red hot! I mean she was
The drink will flow and blood will spill, and if the boys wan - na fight you bet - ter
let ring…
let ring…
A5
C♯m7
D
cats are cra - zy. They were ask - in' if you were a - round,
stea - min'! And that time ov - er at Jon - ny's place,
let 'em. That juke-box in the cor - ner blas - tin' out my fav -'rite song.
Gtr. 3 (2°)
full
let ring…

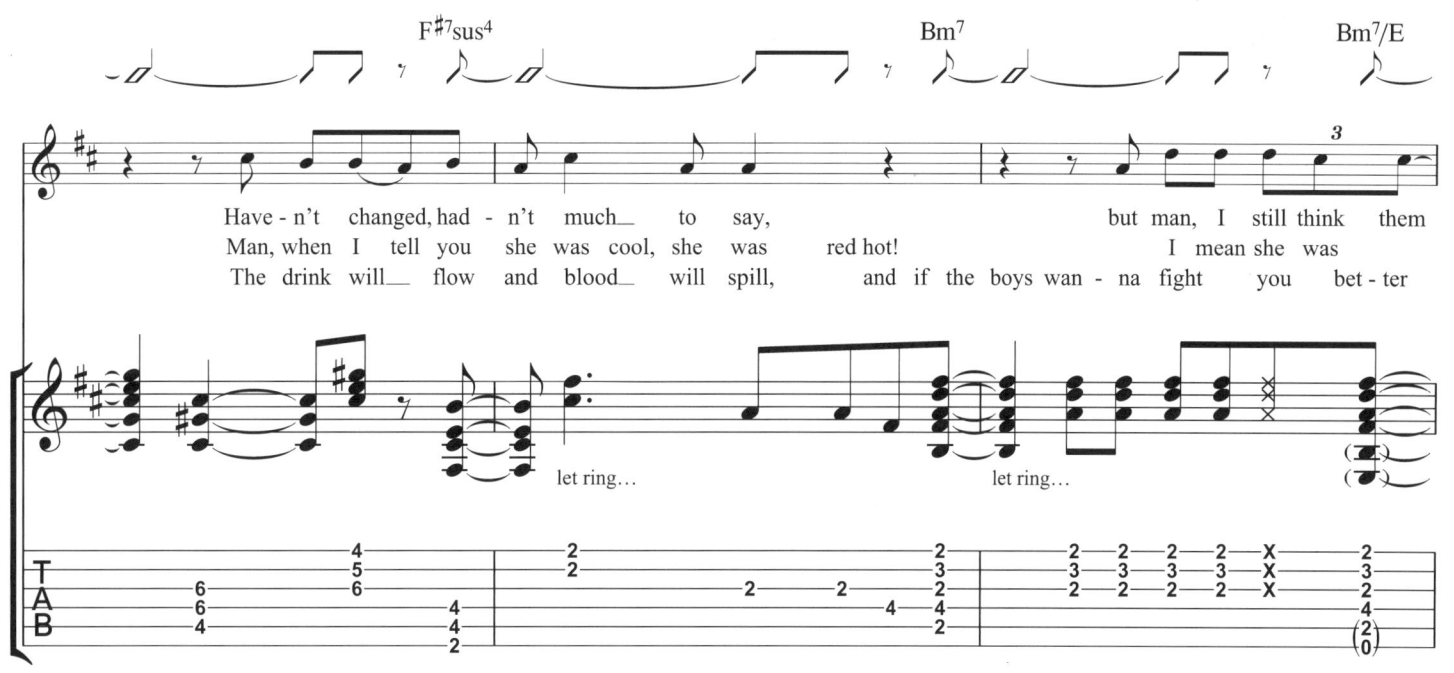

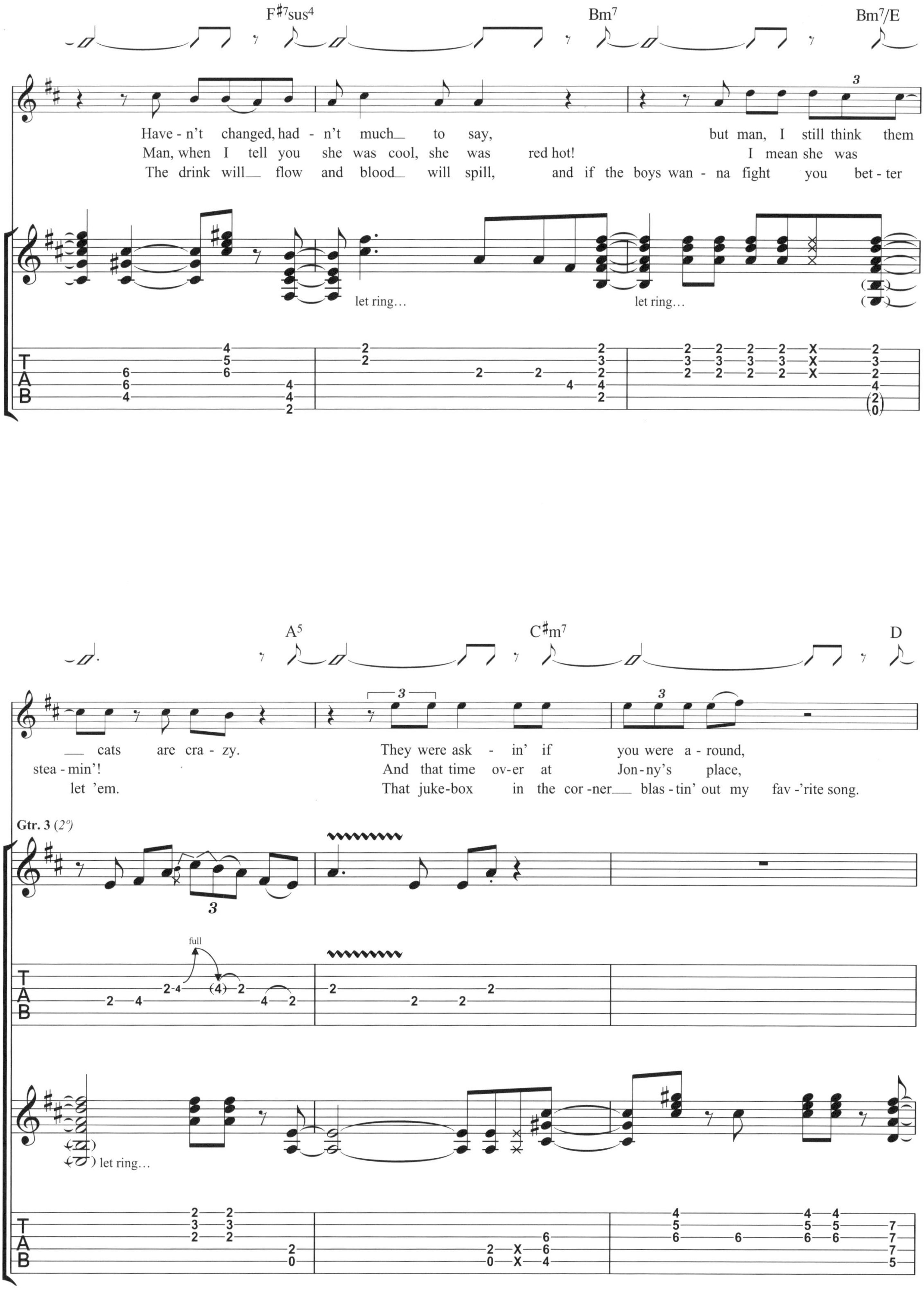

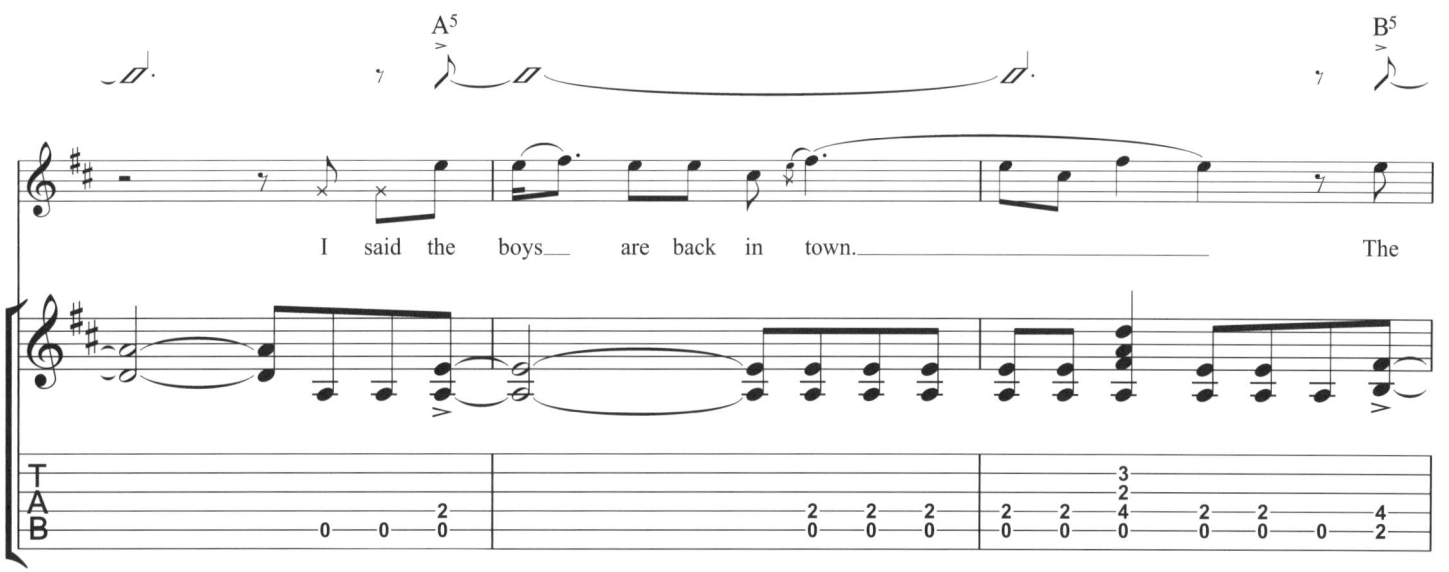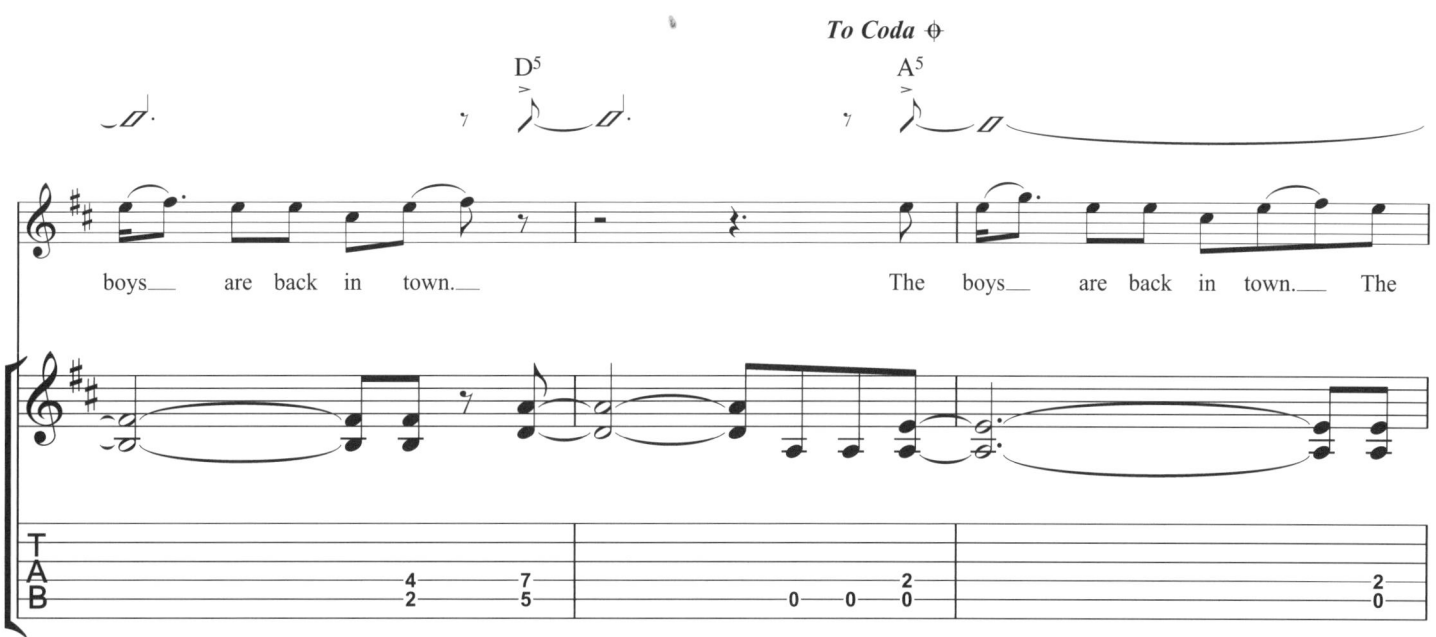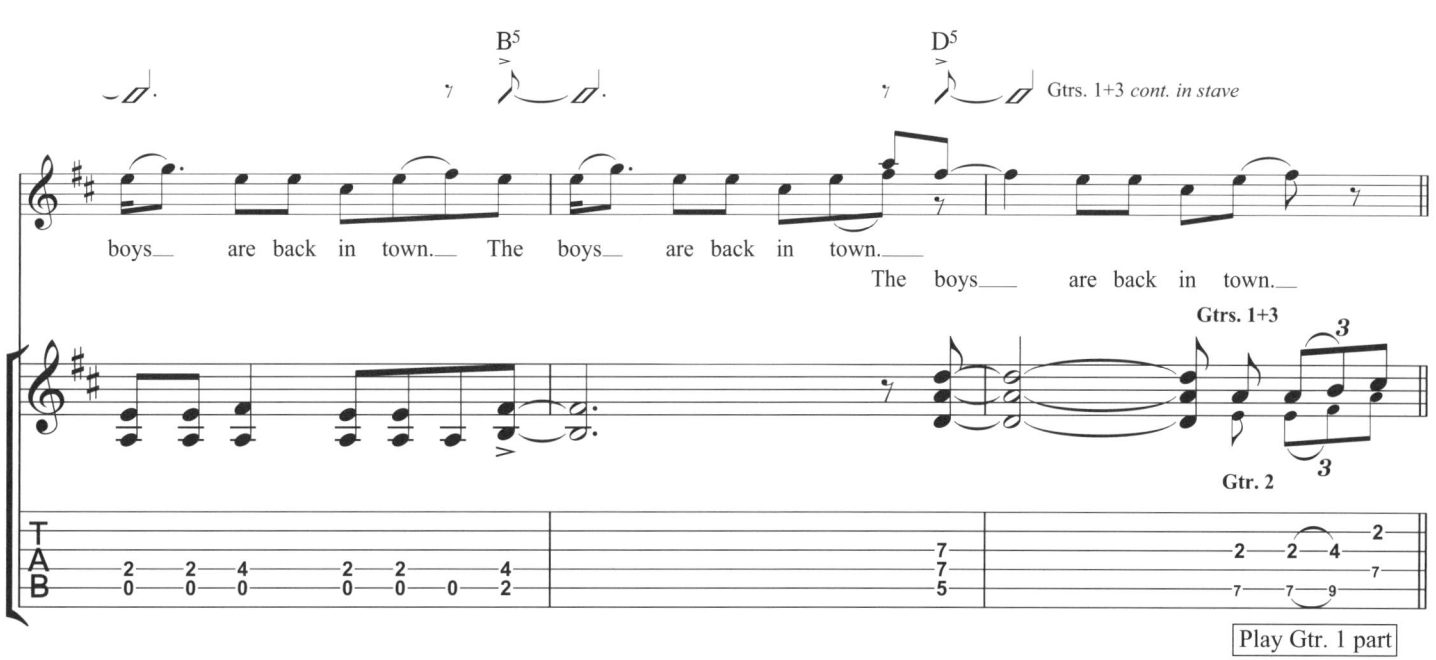

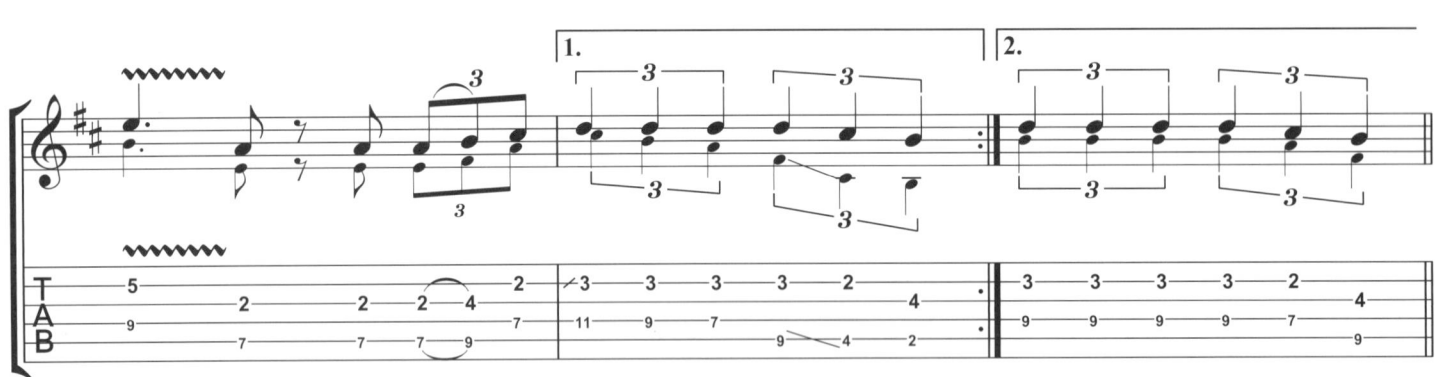

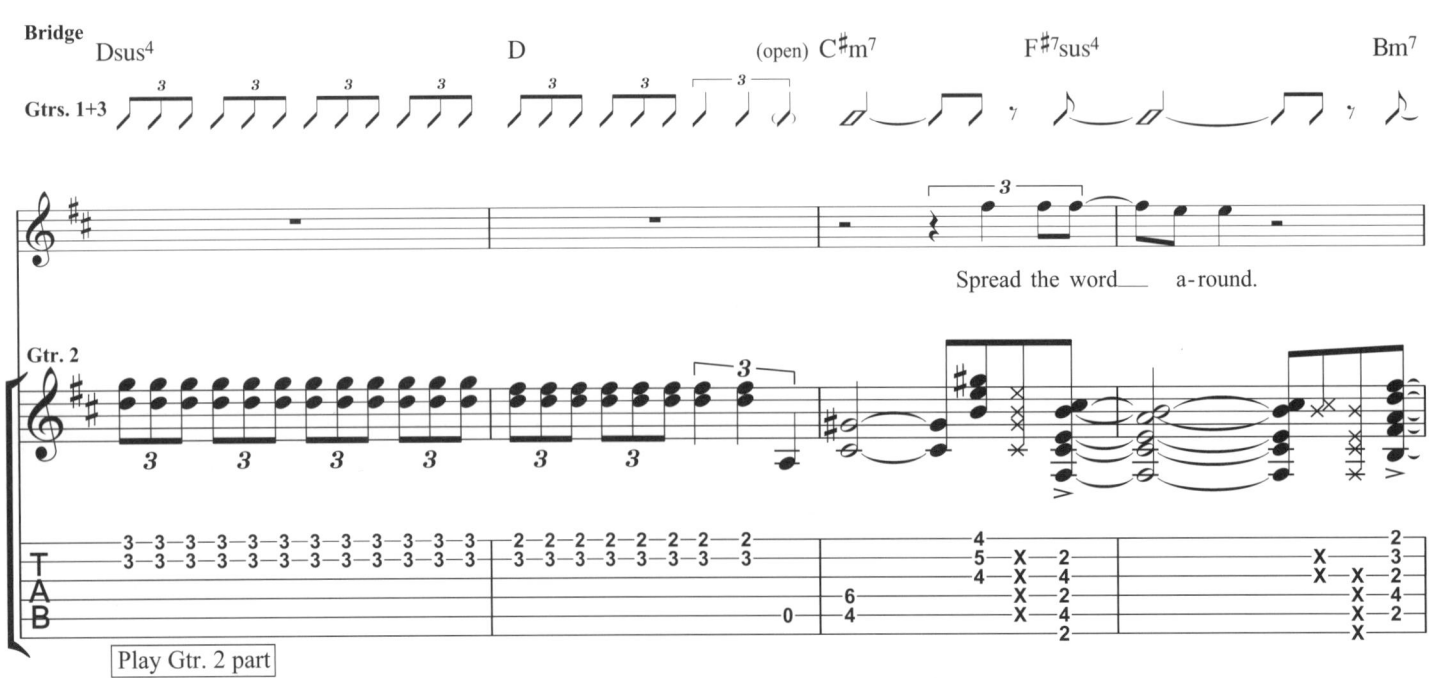

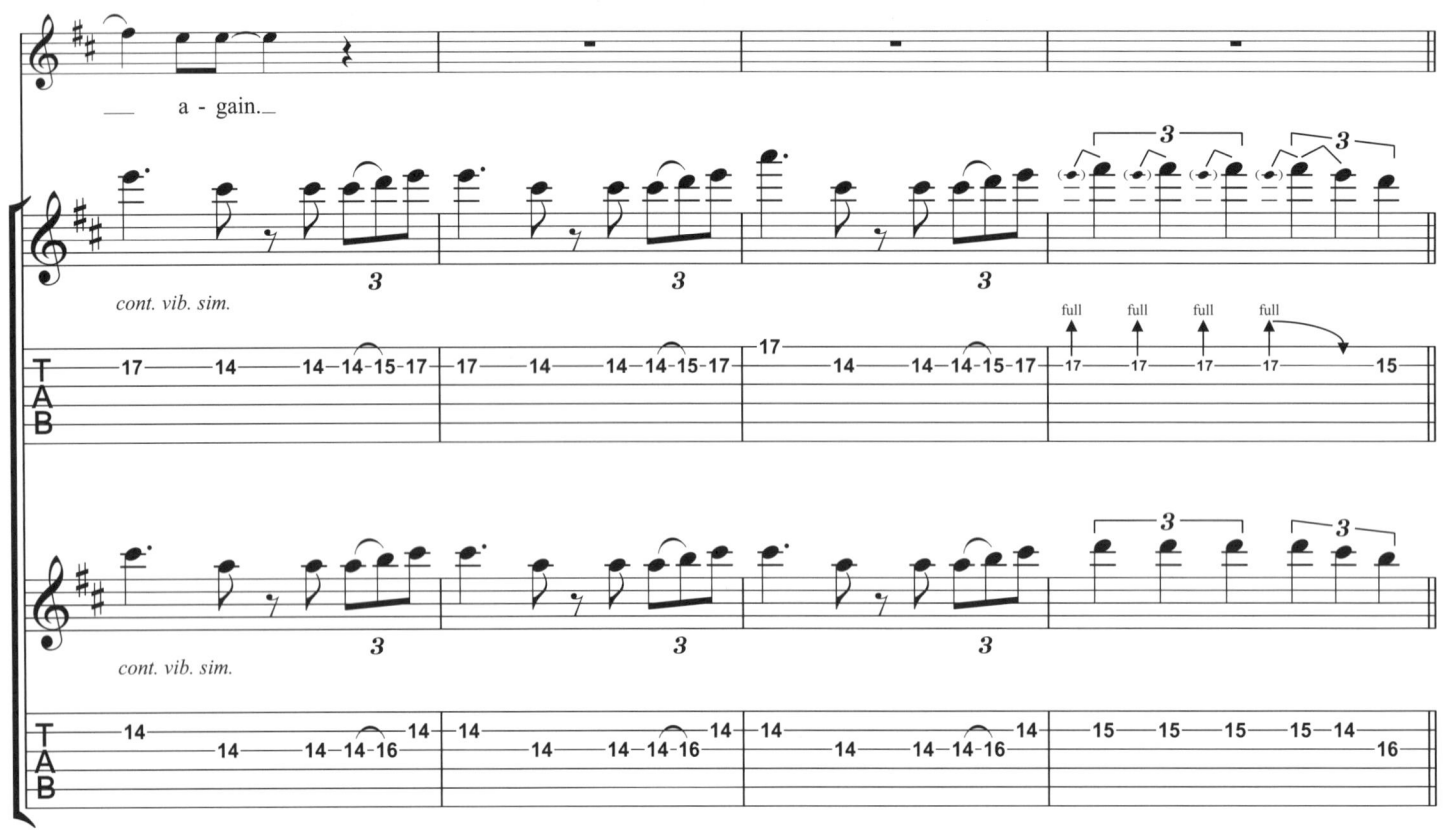
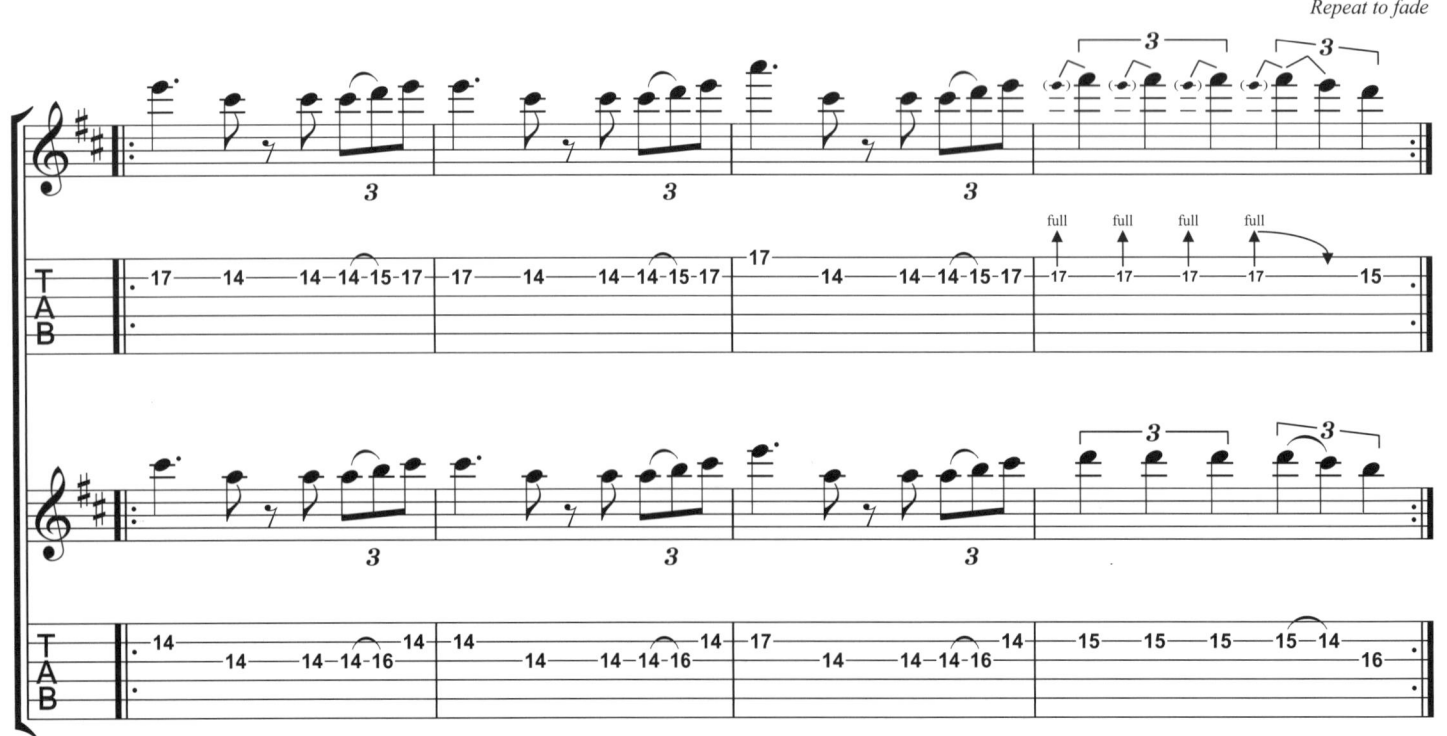

breaking the law

Words and Music by
Glenn Tipton, Rob Halford & K.K. Downing

© Copyright 1980 EMI April Music Incorporated/Ebonytree Limited/Geargate Limited/Crewglen Limited.
EMI Songs Limited.
All Rights Reserved. International Copyright Secured.

Full performance demo: track 3
Backing only: track 10

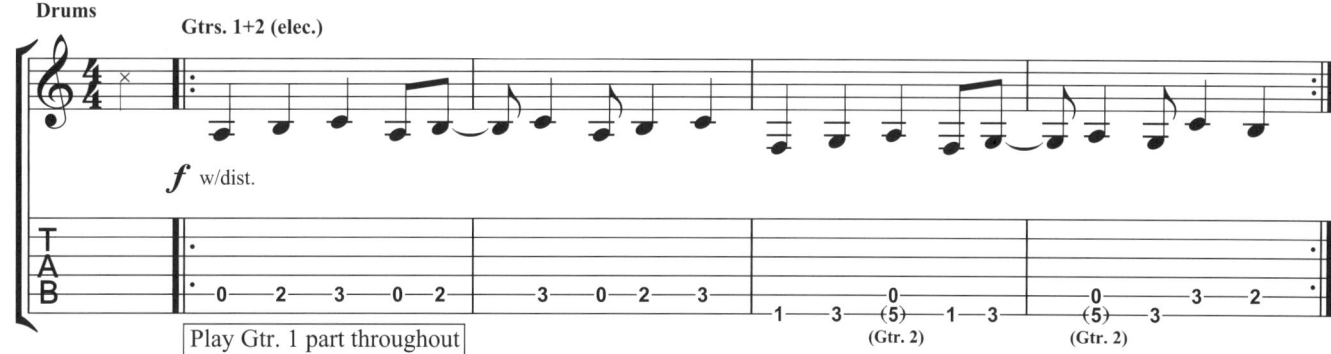

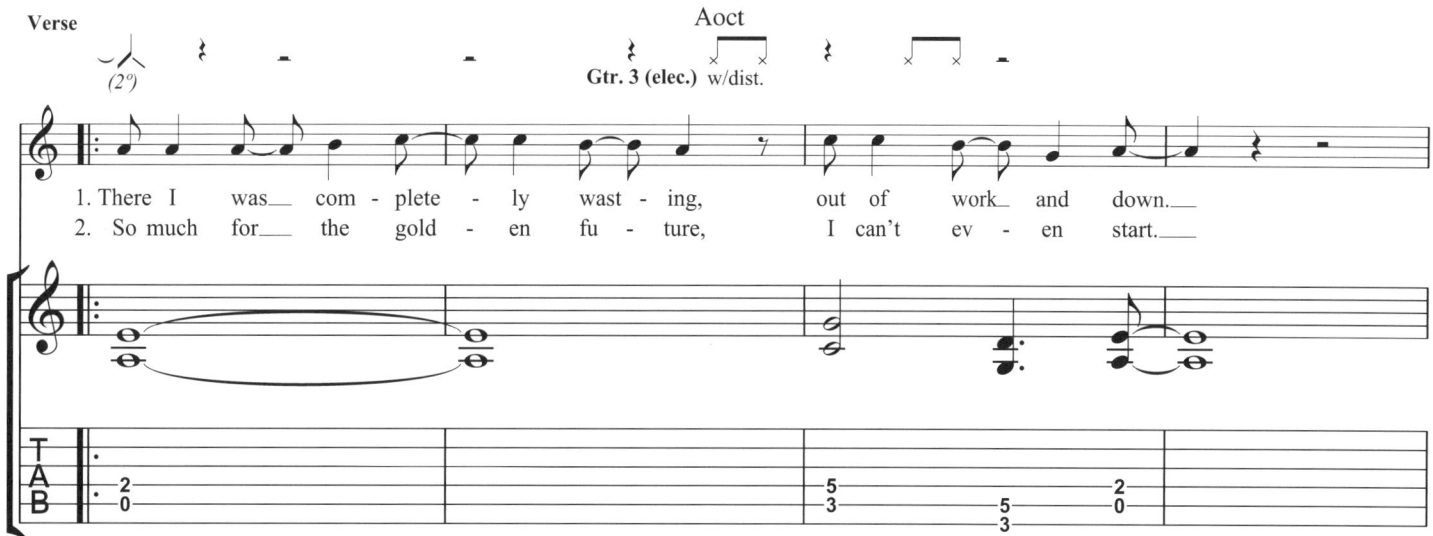

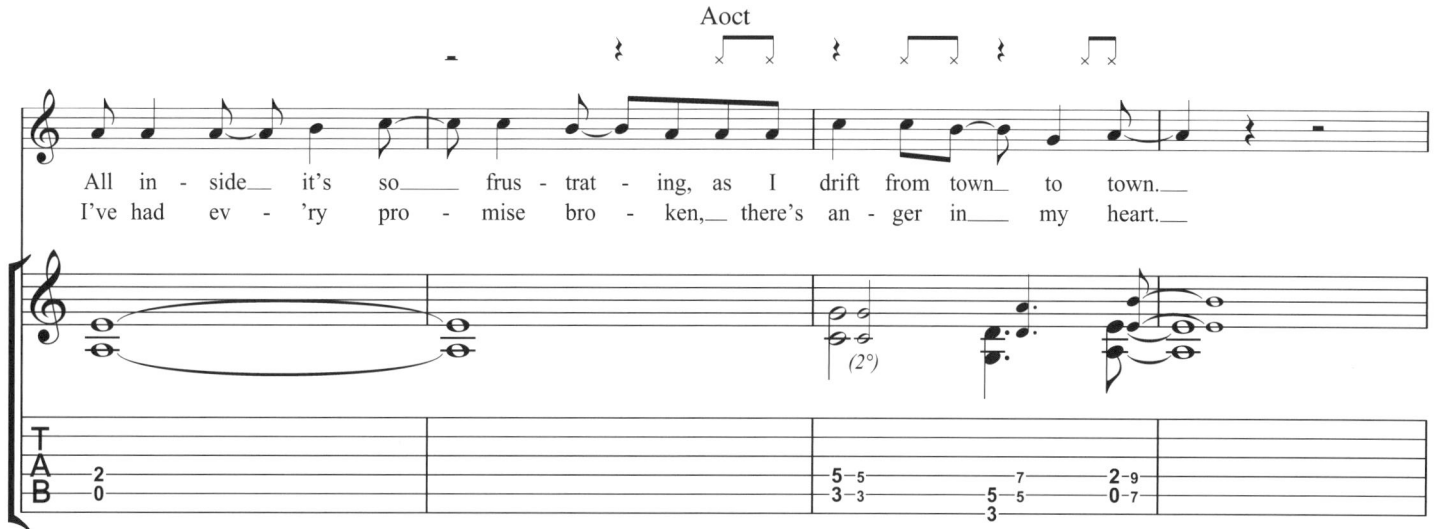

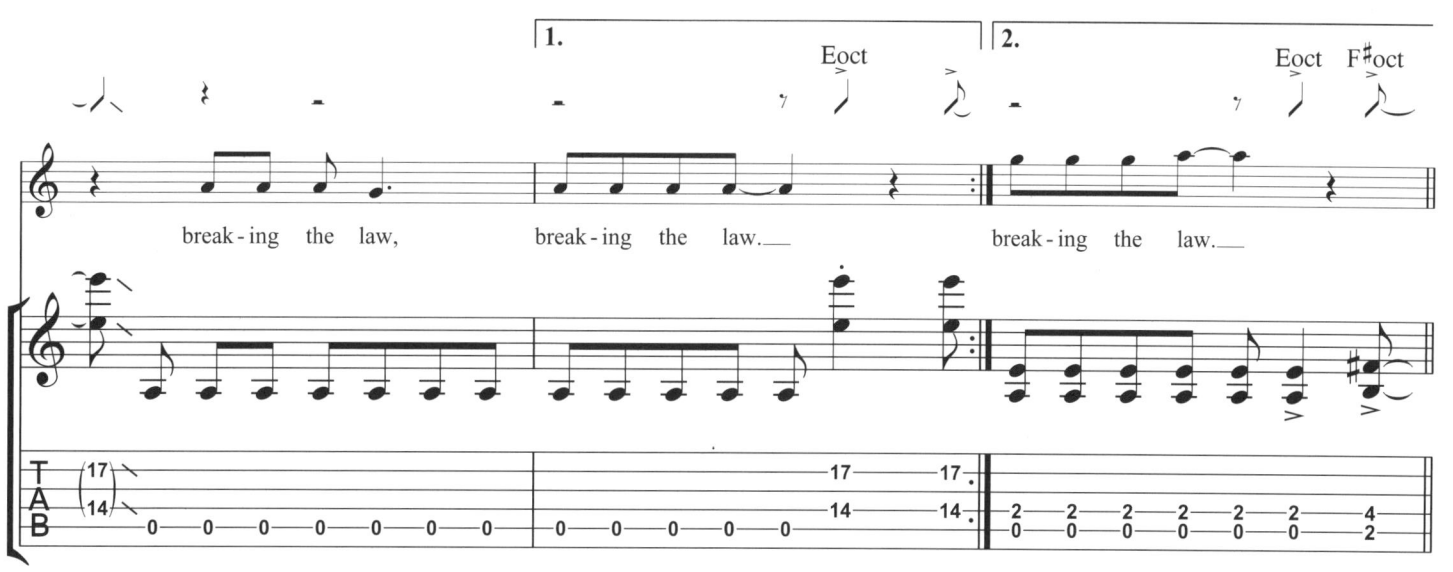
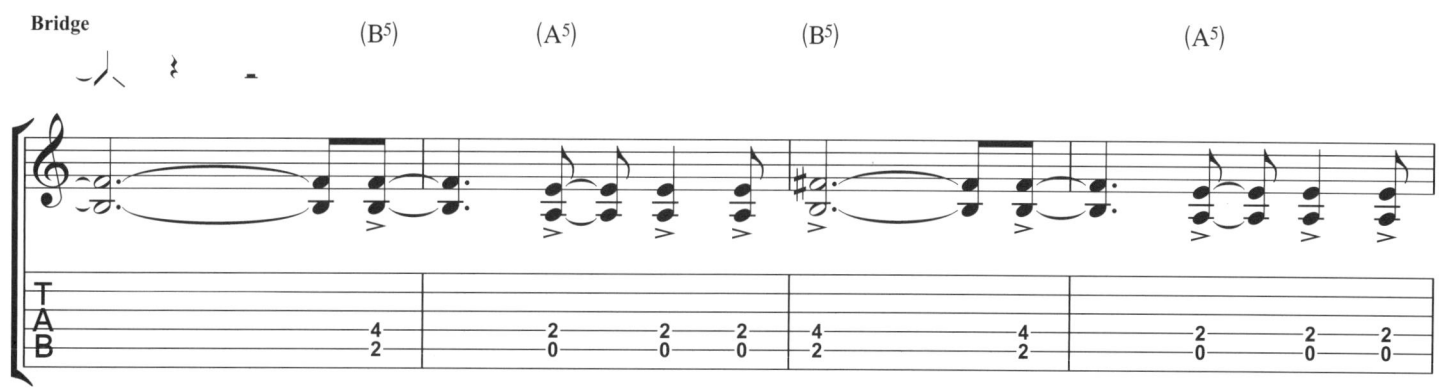
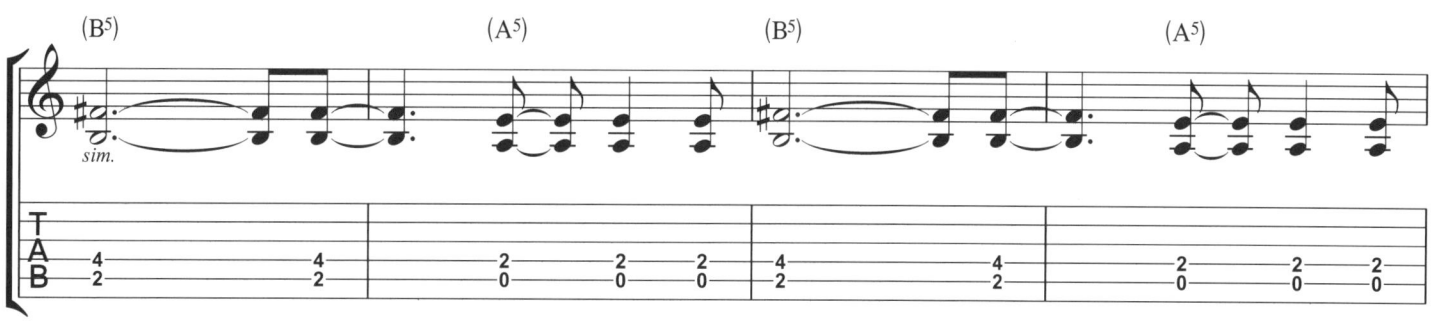
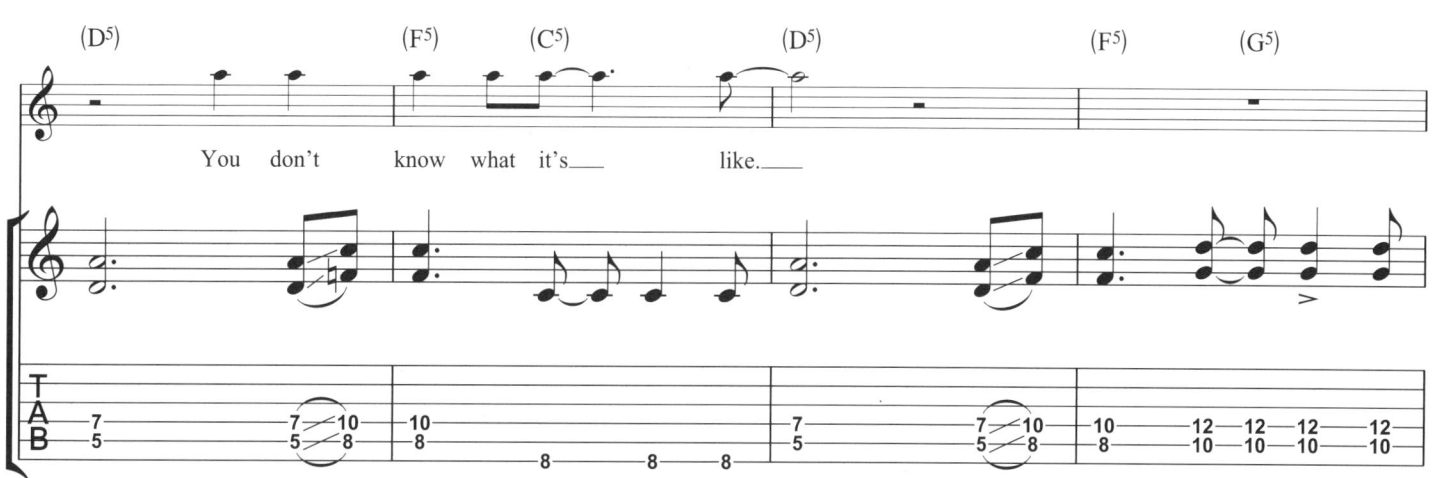

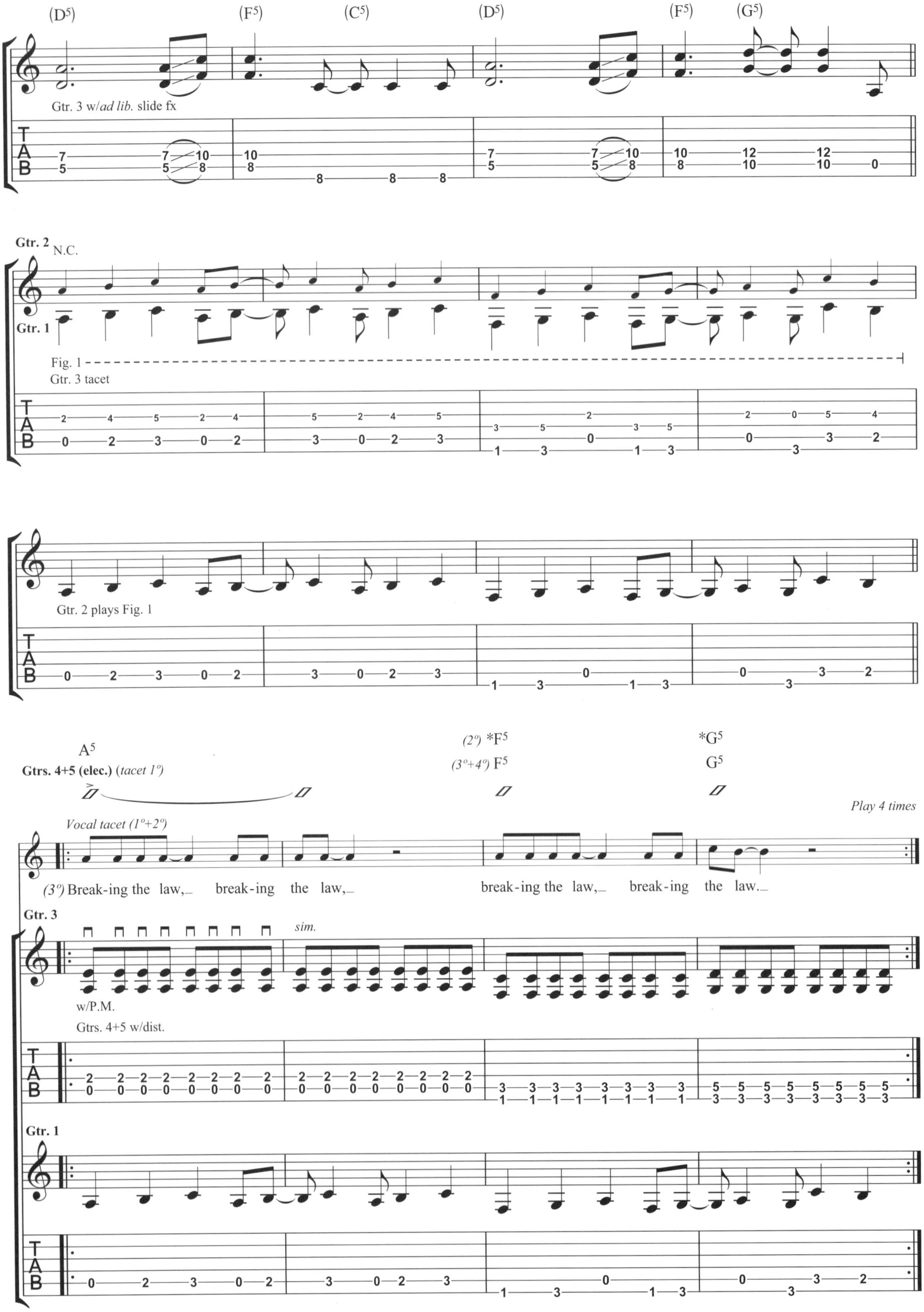
(D5) (F5) (C5) (D5) (F5) (G5)
Gtr. 3 w/ad lib. slide fx
Gtr. 2 N.C.
Gtr. 1
Fig. 1
Gtr. 3 tacet
Gtr. 2 plays Fig. 1
A5
Gtrs. 4+5 (elec.) (tacet 1º)
(2º) *F5
(3º+4º) F5
*G5
G5
Play 4 times
Vocal tacet (1º+2º)
(3º) Break-ing the law, break-ing the law, break-ing the law, break-ing the law.
Gtr. 3
sim.
w/P.M.
Gtrs. 4+5 w/dist.
Gtr. 1

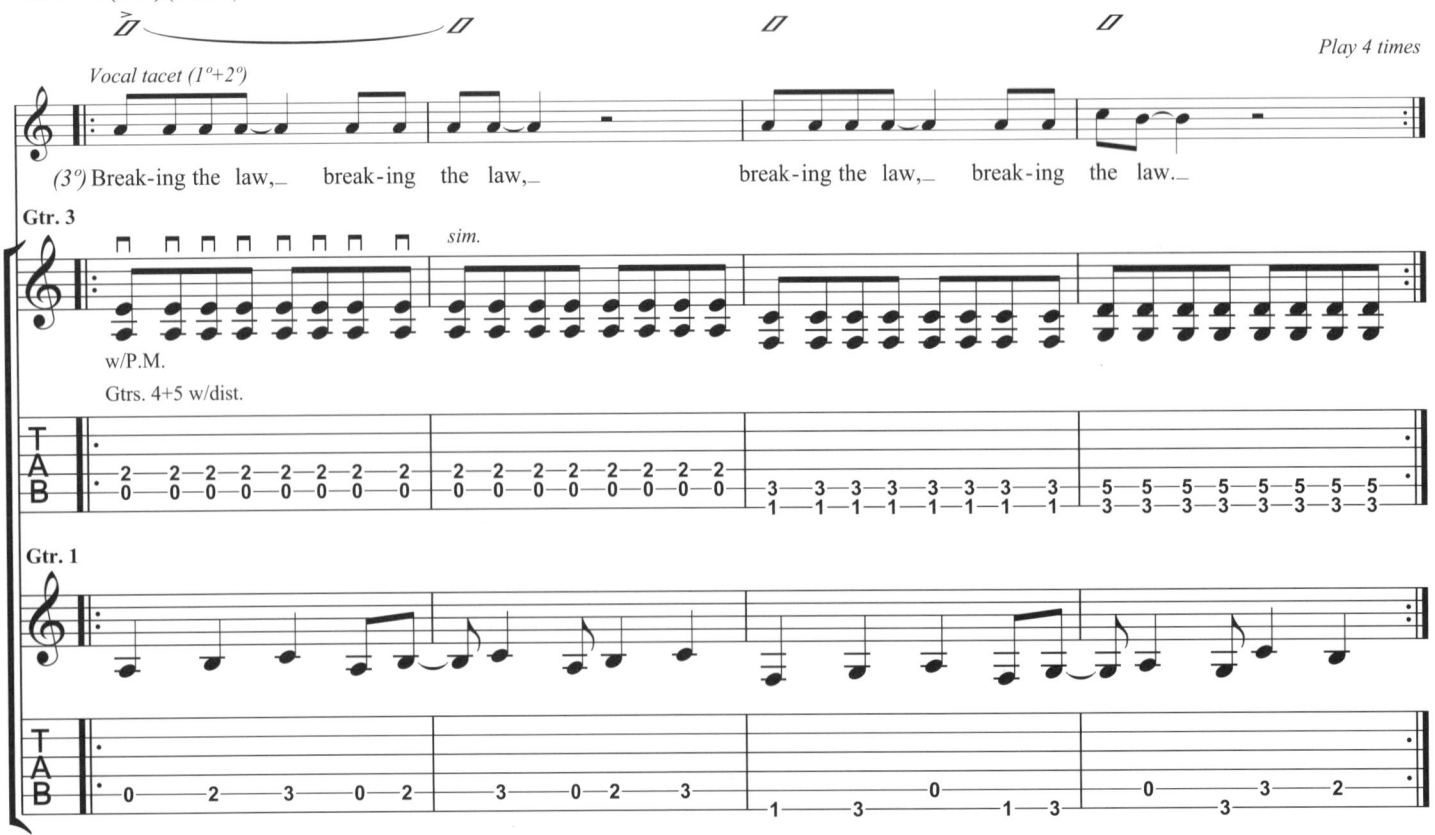

A5
F5
G5
Breaking the law, breaking the law, breaking the law, breaking
Gtr. 2 plays sim. 8va
1.
2.
G5
A5
G5
A5
ing the law.
ing the law.

the number of the beast

**Words and Music by
Steve Harris**

© Copyright 1982 Imagem Music.
All Rights Reserved. International Copyright Secured.

Full performance demo: track 4
Backing only: track 11

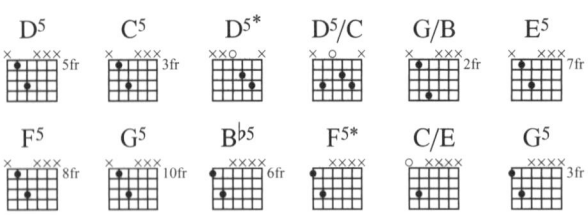

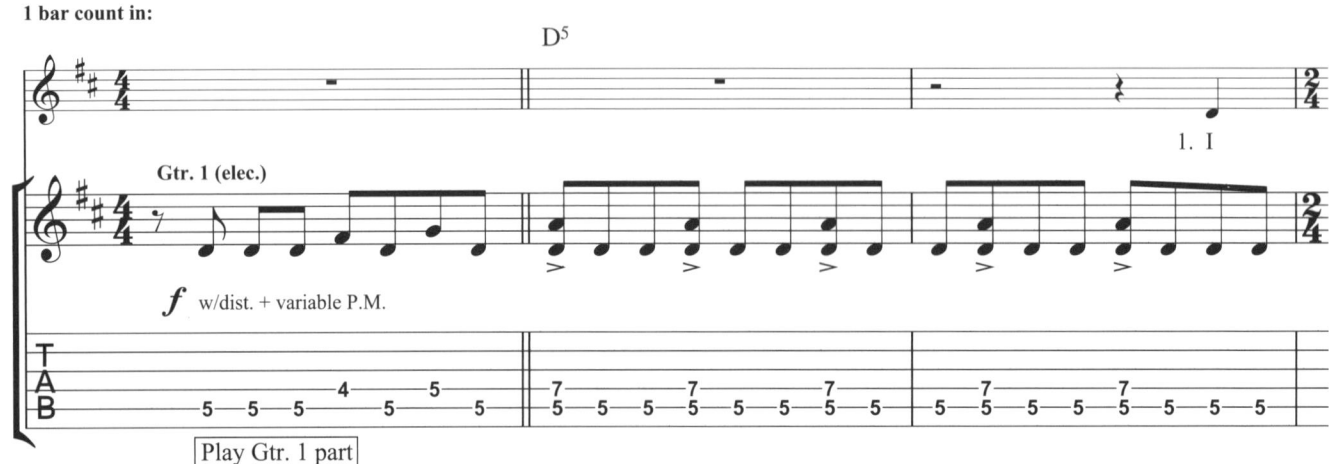

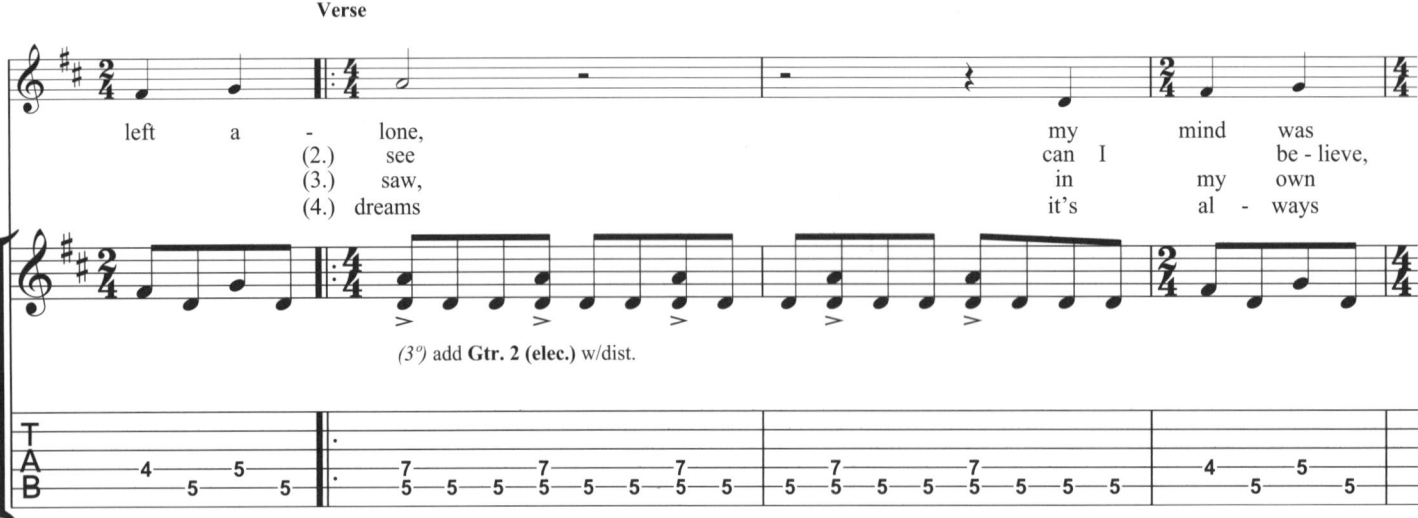

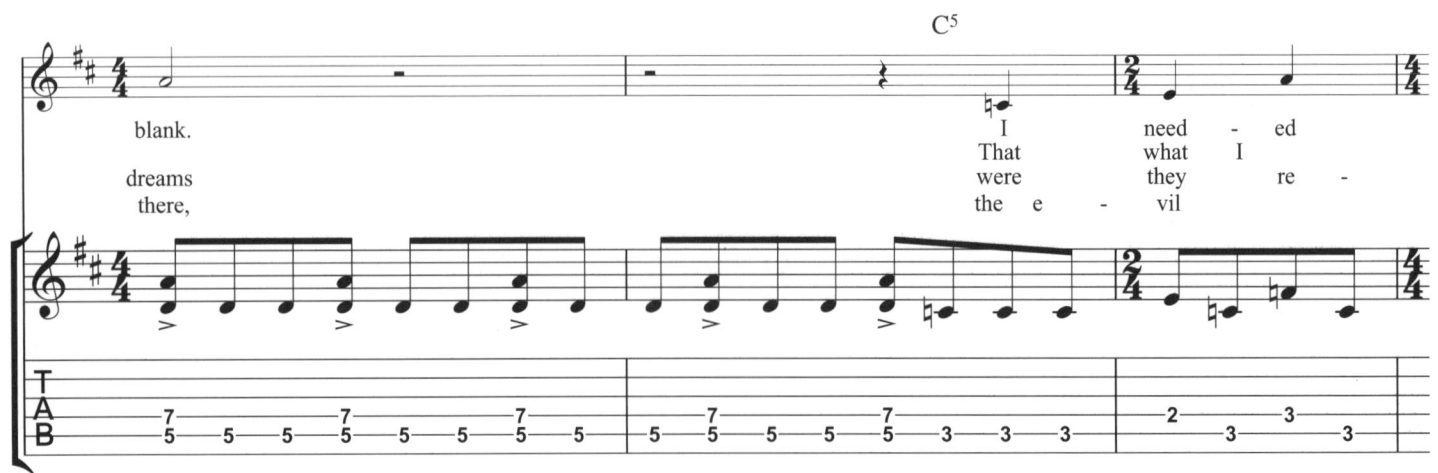

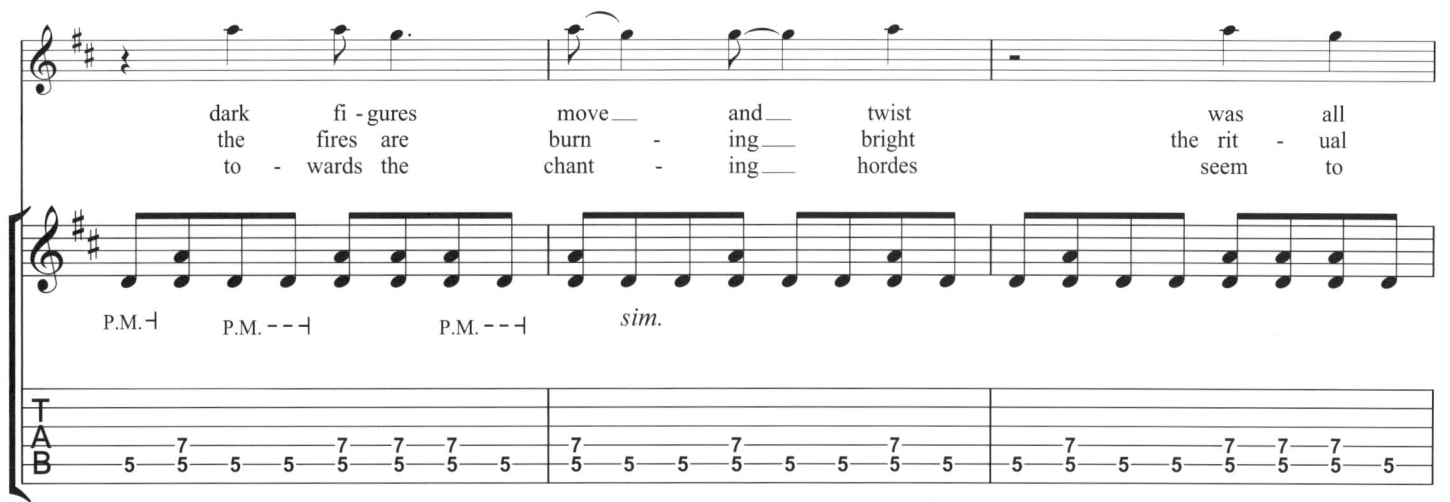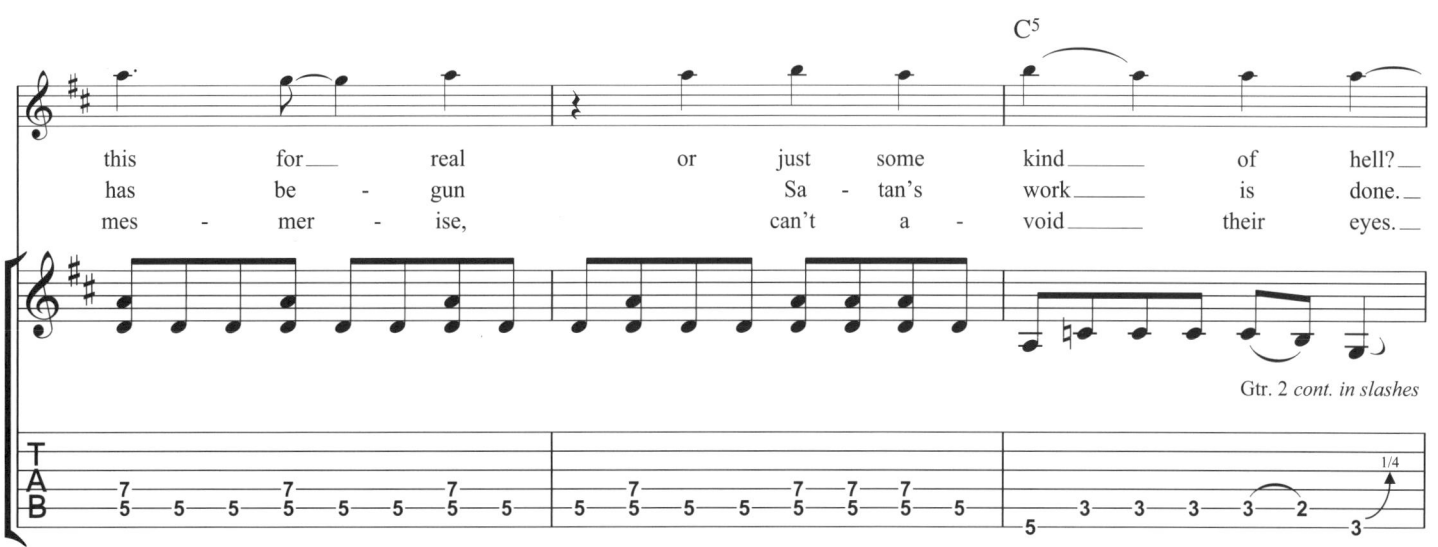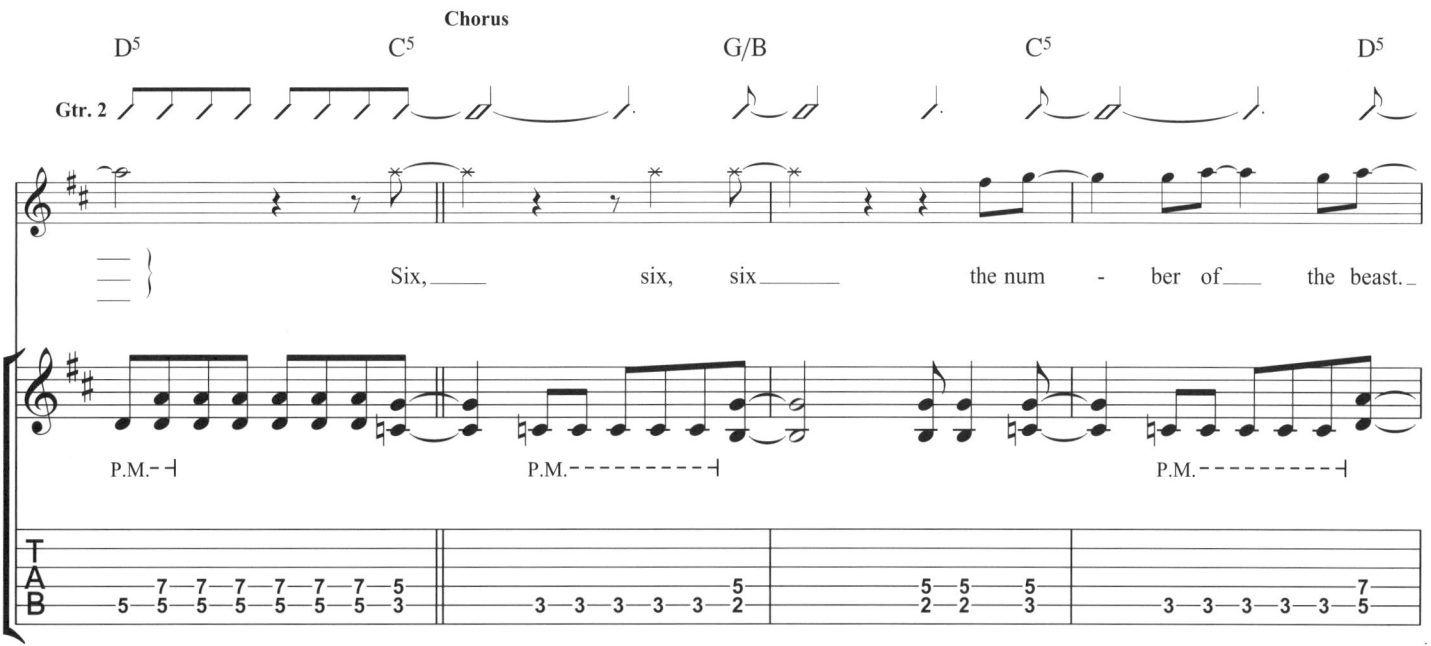

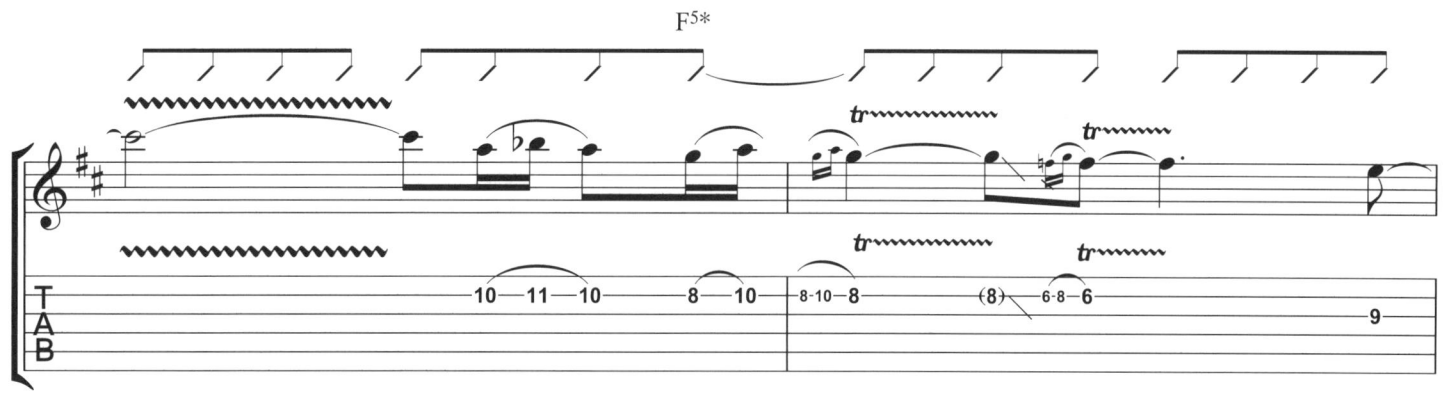
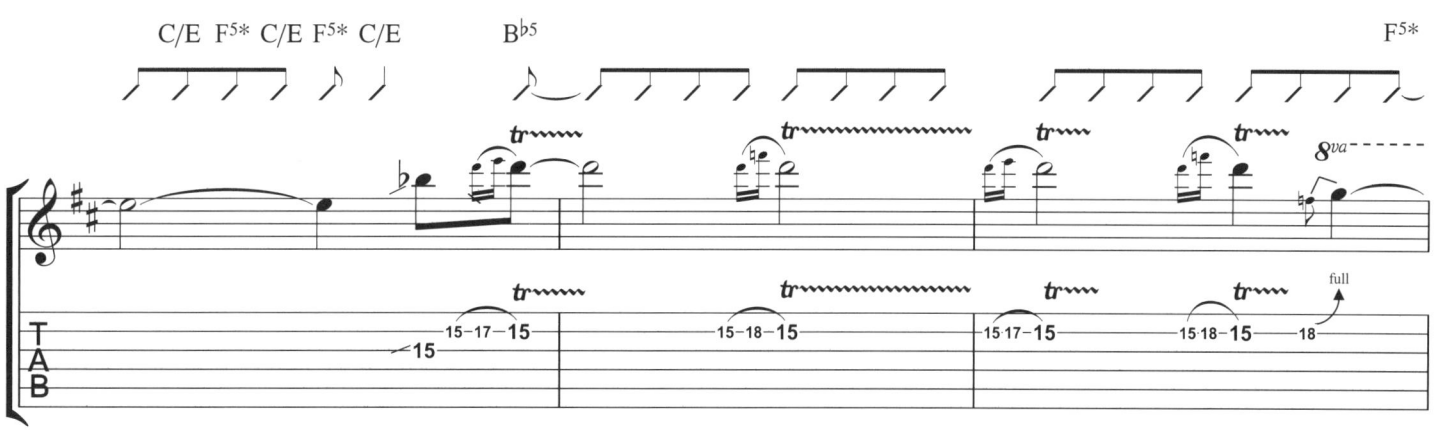
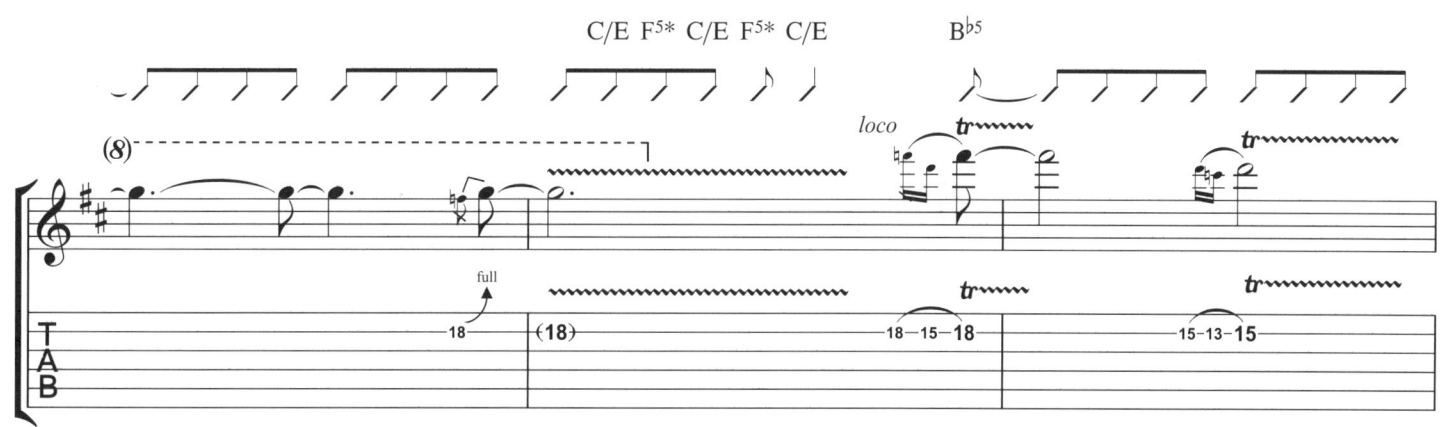

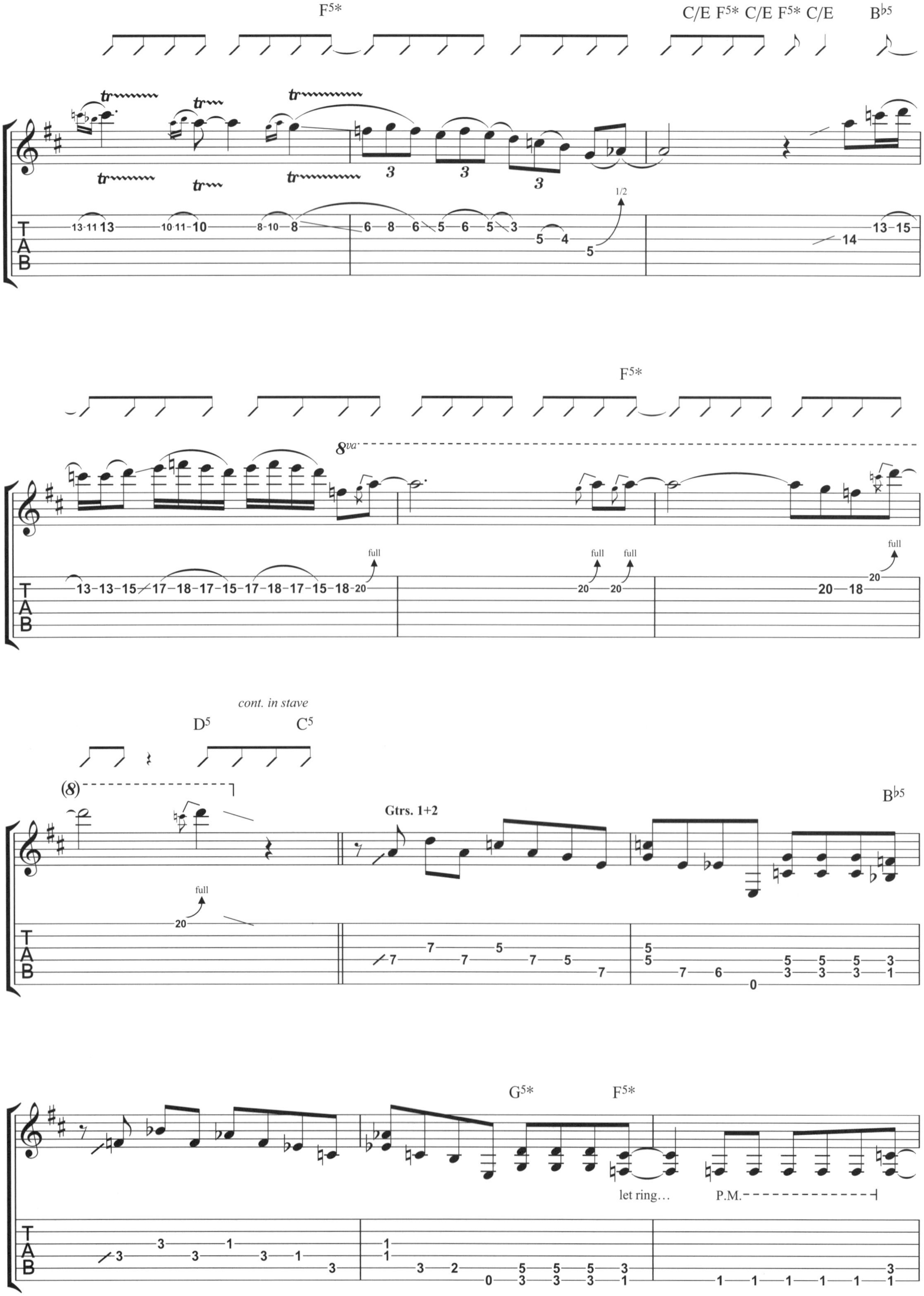

F5*
C/E F5* C/E F5* C/E
B♭5
1/2
F5*
8va
full
cont. in stave
D5
C5
(8)
Gtrs. 1+2
B♭5
G5*
F5*
let ring…
P.M.

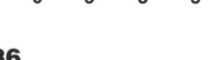

G5
A5
C5
D5
Gtr. 1
P.M.
Solo
F5
G5
B♭5
Gtr. 2
full
1/4
Play Gtr. 2 part
C5
D5
F5
G5
B♭5
1/2

G5 B♭5 C5 D5
full full full full
* full full full full full
* bends are approximate
F5 G5 B♭5
8va
full full
8va
full full
C5 D5 F5 G5
(8)
B♭5 C5 D5 F5

G5
B♭5
C5
D.S. al Coda
7. This
Coda
cont. in stave
D5
for you and me.
8. I'm
w/P.M.
com - ing
back
(9.) fire
I will re - turn
I have the
force
C5
and I'll pos - ess your bo -
I have the power to make

D5
- dy and I'll make you burn.
— my ev - il take its course.
Outro
1.
2.
D5*
9. I have the
P.M.
D5/C
D5*
D5 C5 D5

smoke on the water

Words and Music by
Ian Gillan, Ritchie Blackmore, Jon Lord, Roger Glover & Ian Paice

© Copyright 1972 HEC Music.
All Rights Reserved. International Copyright Secured.

Full performance demo: track 5
Backing only: track 12

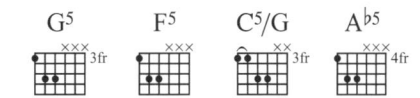

But Frank Zap-pa and the Mo - thers were at the best place a - round.
When it all was o - ver, we had to find a - noth - er place,
few red lights, a few old beds, we made a place to sweat.

But some stu - pid with a flare gun burned the place to the ground.
but Swiss time was run - ning out, it seemed that we would lose the race.
No mat - ter what we get of this, I know, I know we'll nev - er for - get.

Chorus

Smoke on the wa - ter, a fire in the sky. Smoke on the

wa - ter,

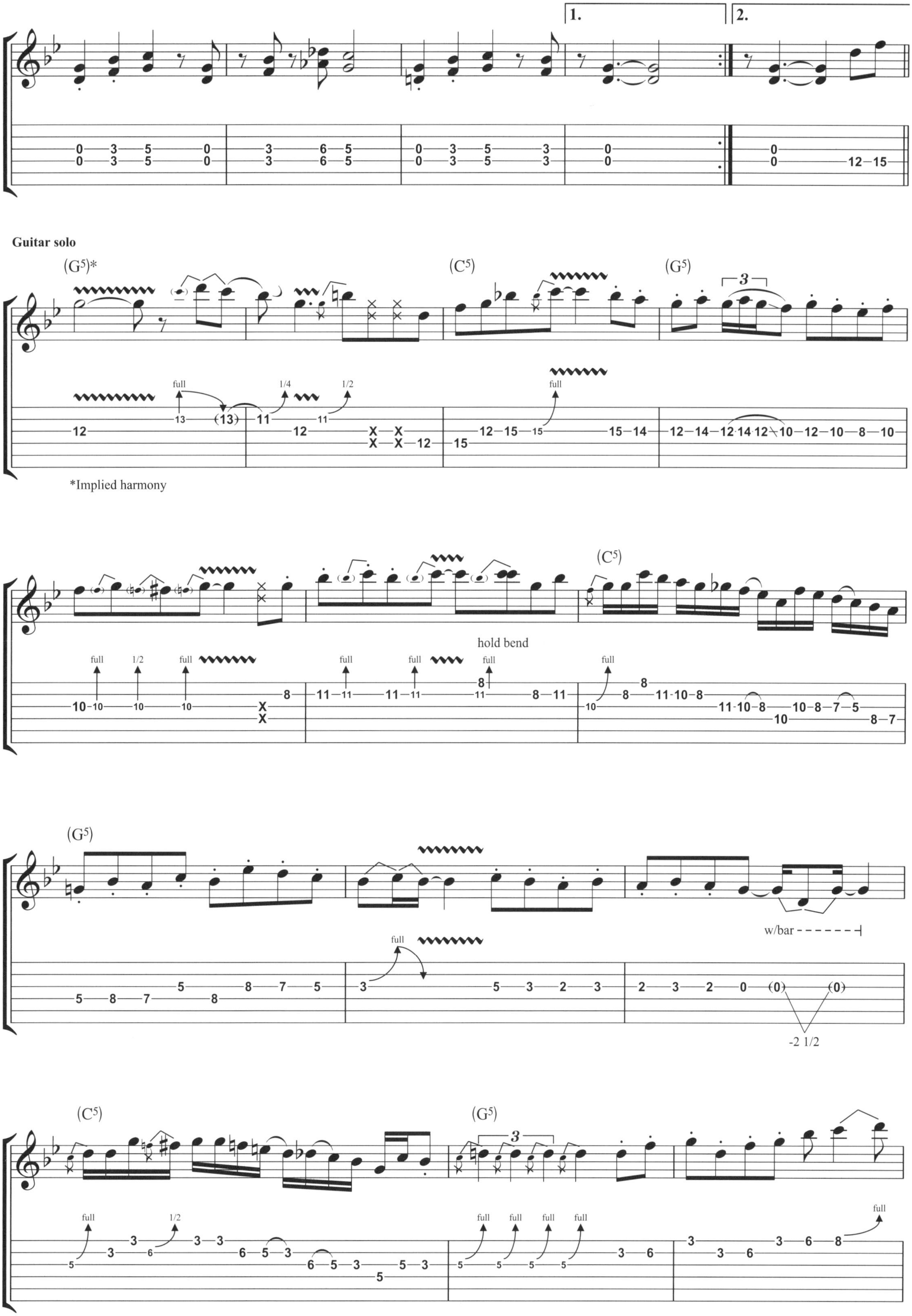
1.
2.
Guitar solo
(G5)*
(C5)
(G5)
full
1/4
1/2
*Implied harmony
hold bend
w/bar
-2 1/2

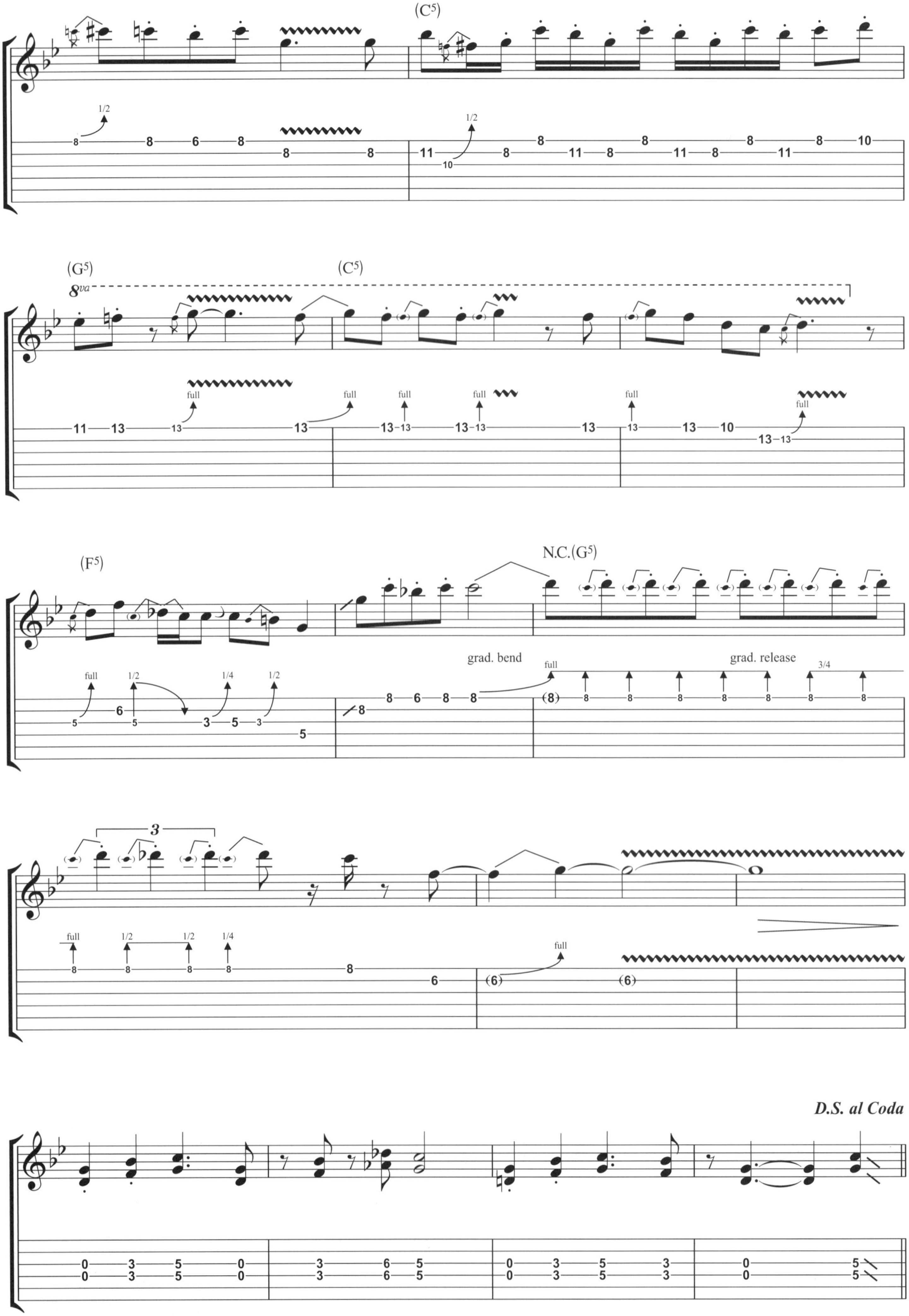
(C5)
(G5)
8va
(C5)
(F5)
N.C.(G5)
grad. bend
grad. release
D.S. al Coda

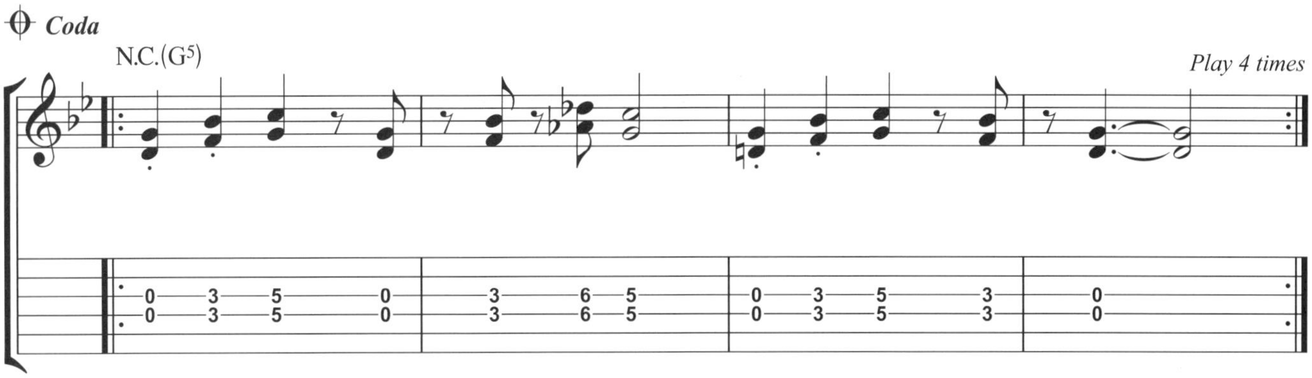

Outro
Organ solo

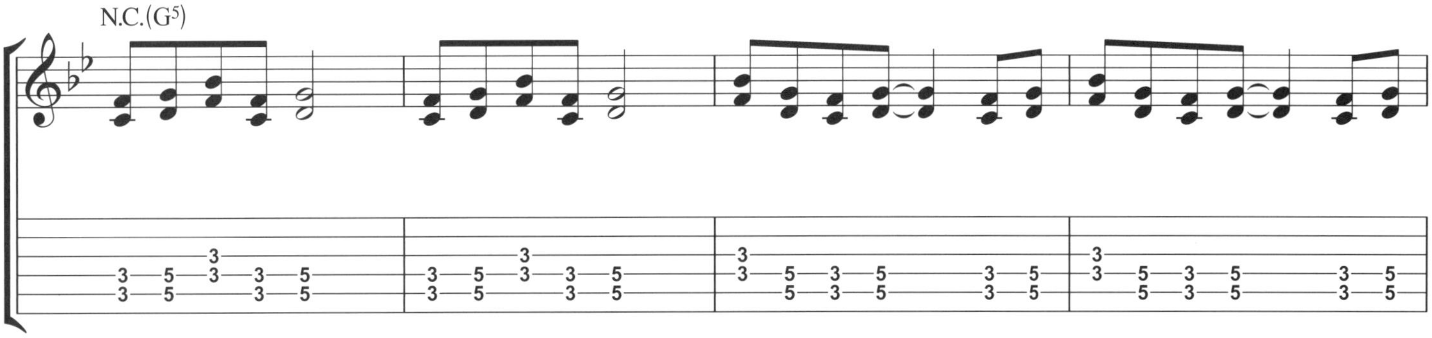

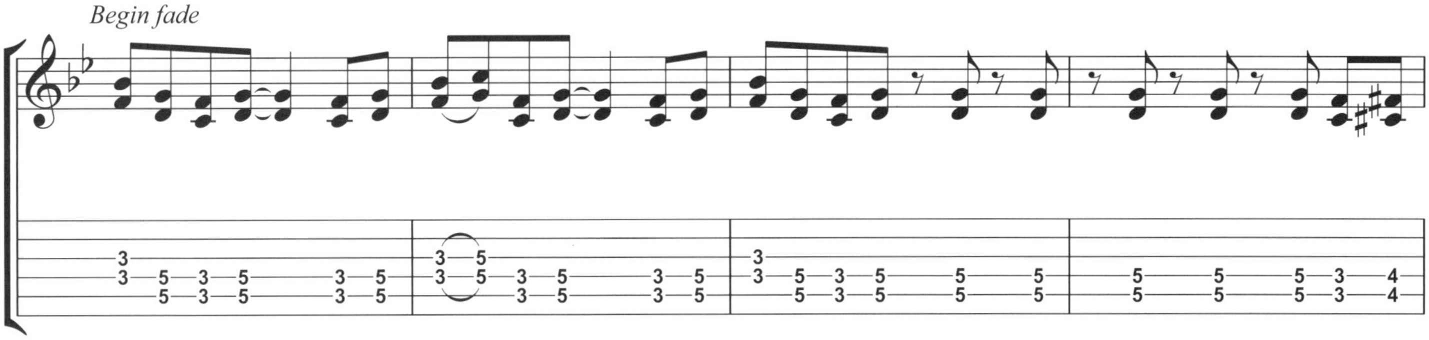

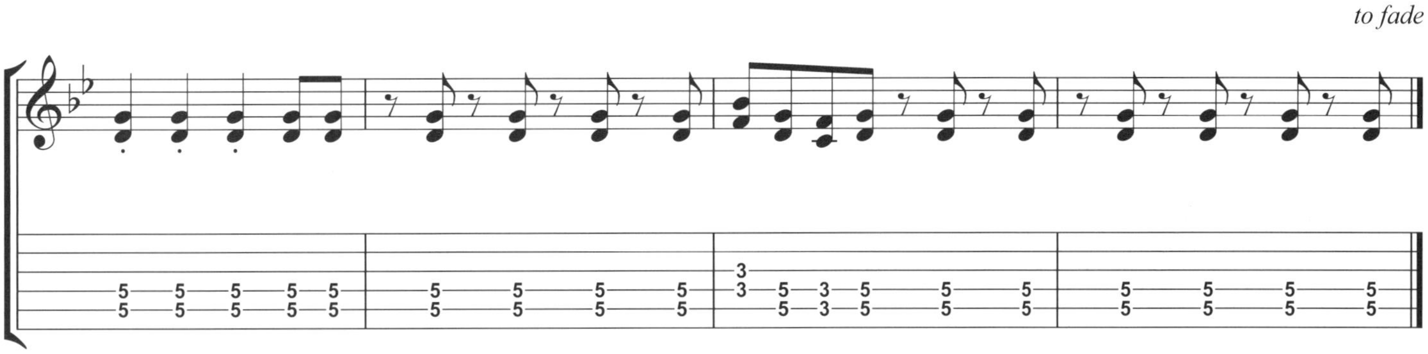

paranoid

Words and Music by
Ozzy Osbourne, Tony Iommi, Terry 'Geezer' Butler & Bill Ward

© Copyright 1970 Westminster Music Limited.
All Rights Reserved. International Copyright Secured.

Full performance demo: track 6
Backing only: track 13

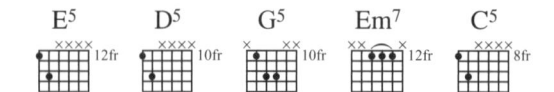

Chord diagrams: E5 (12fr), D5 (10fr), G5 (10fr), Em7 (12fr), C5 (8fr)

Intro
2 bar count in:

♩ = 165

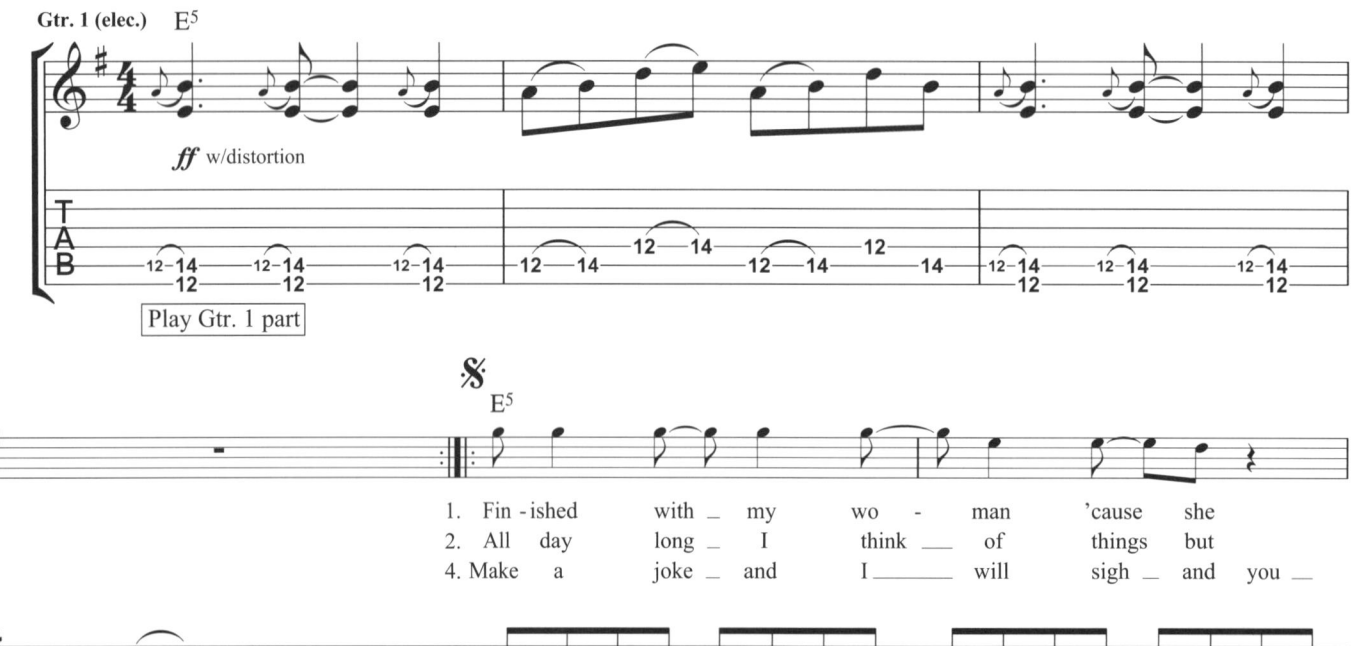

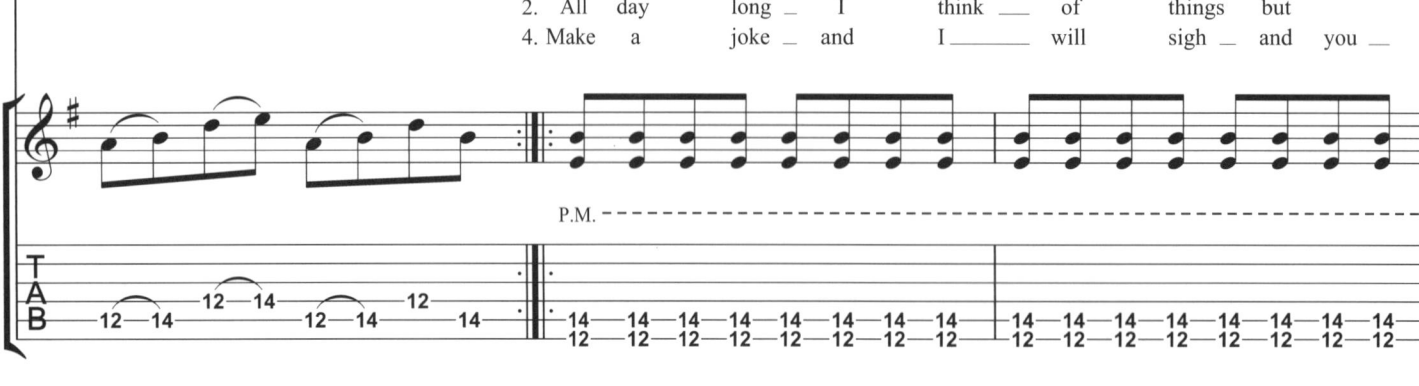

Gtr. 1 (elec.)   E5

ff w/distortion

Play Gtr. 1 part

1. Fin-ished with my wo-man 'cause she
2. All day long I think of things but
4. Make a joke and I will sigh and you

P.M.

could-n't help me with my mind, peo-ple think I'm in
no-thing seems to sa-tis-fy, think I'll lose my mind
you will laugh and I will cry, hap-pi-ness I can

P.M. ———————————| *P.M. sim.*

46

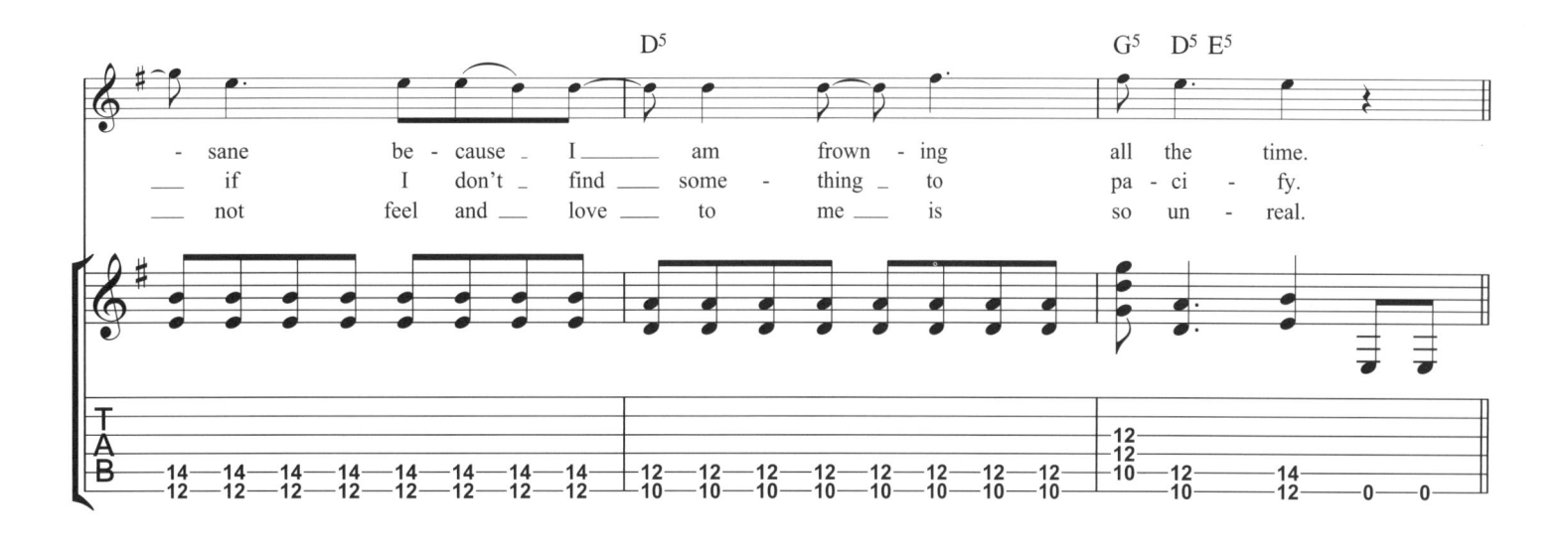

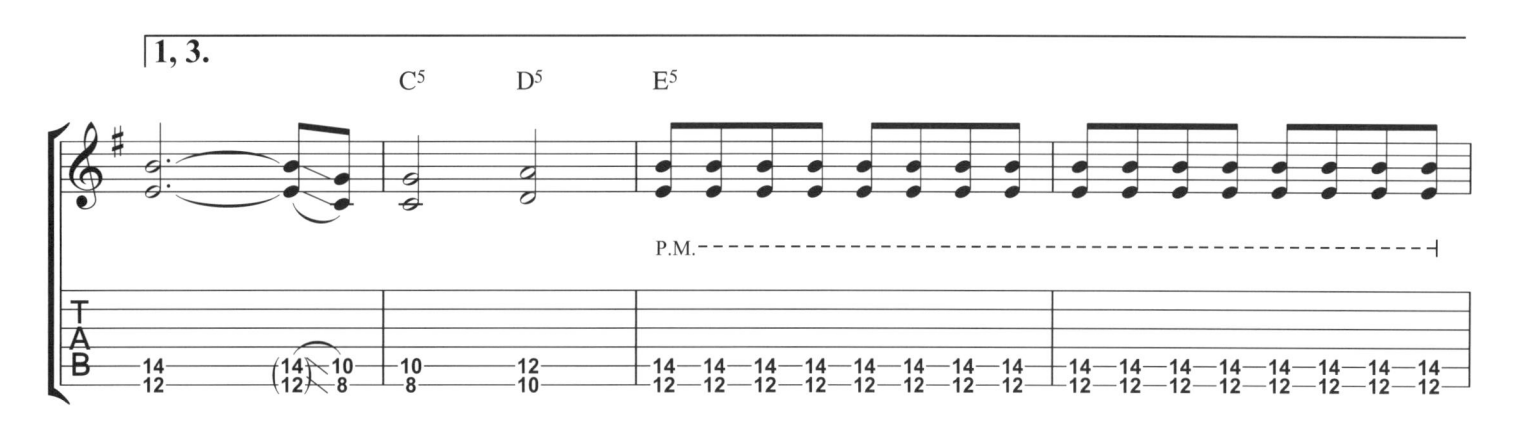

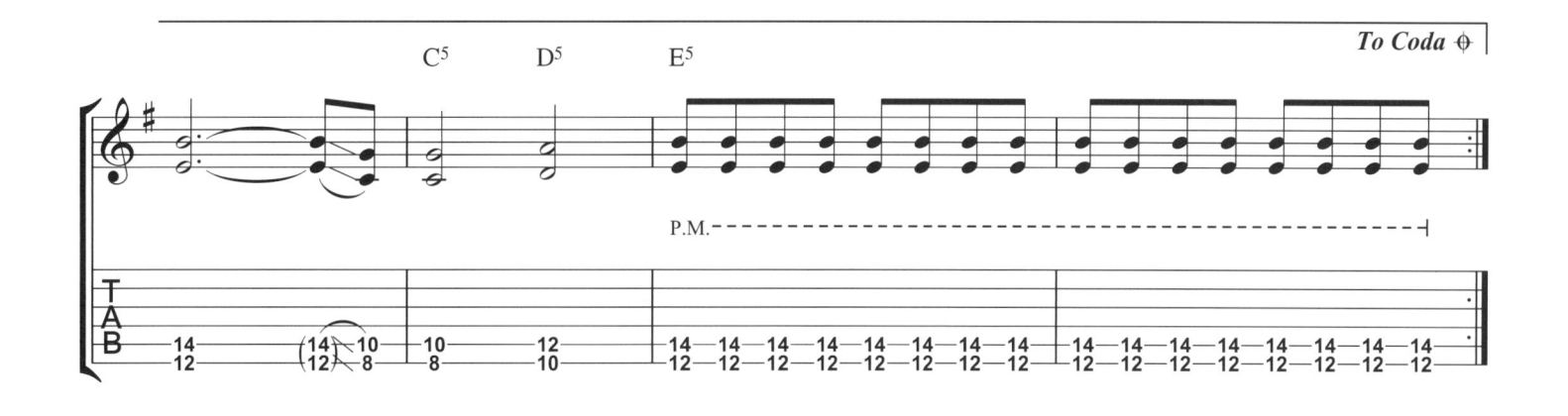

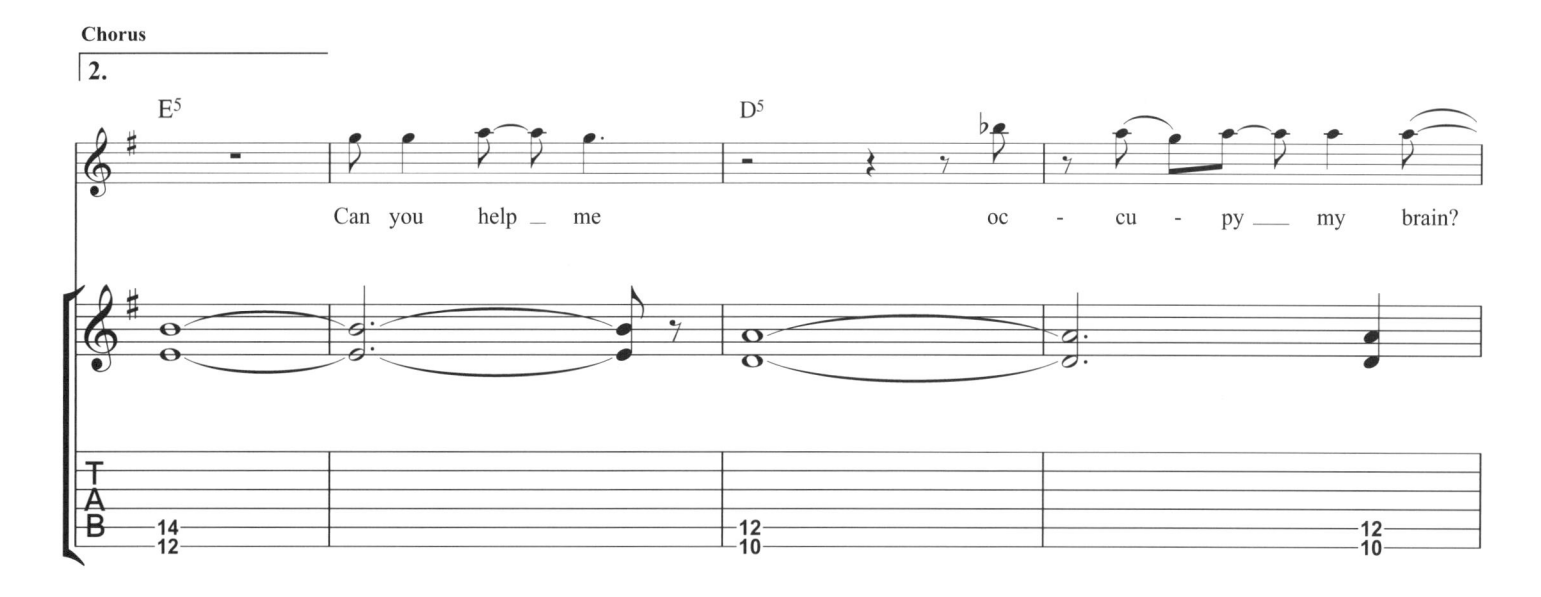

-sane be-cause I am frown-ing all the time.
if I don't find some-thing to pa-ci-fy.
not feel and love to me is so un-real.

1, 3.

To Coda

Chorus
2.

Can you help me oc-cu-py my brain?

E5
D5
Oh yeah.
E5
D5
P.M. sim.
G5 D5 E5 Em7
Verse
E5
3. I need some - one to show me the things
D5
in life that I can't find.
G5 D5 E5 Em7
E5
I can't see the things
Fig. 1

that make true happiness, I must be blind.

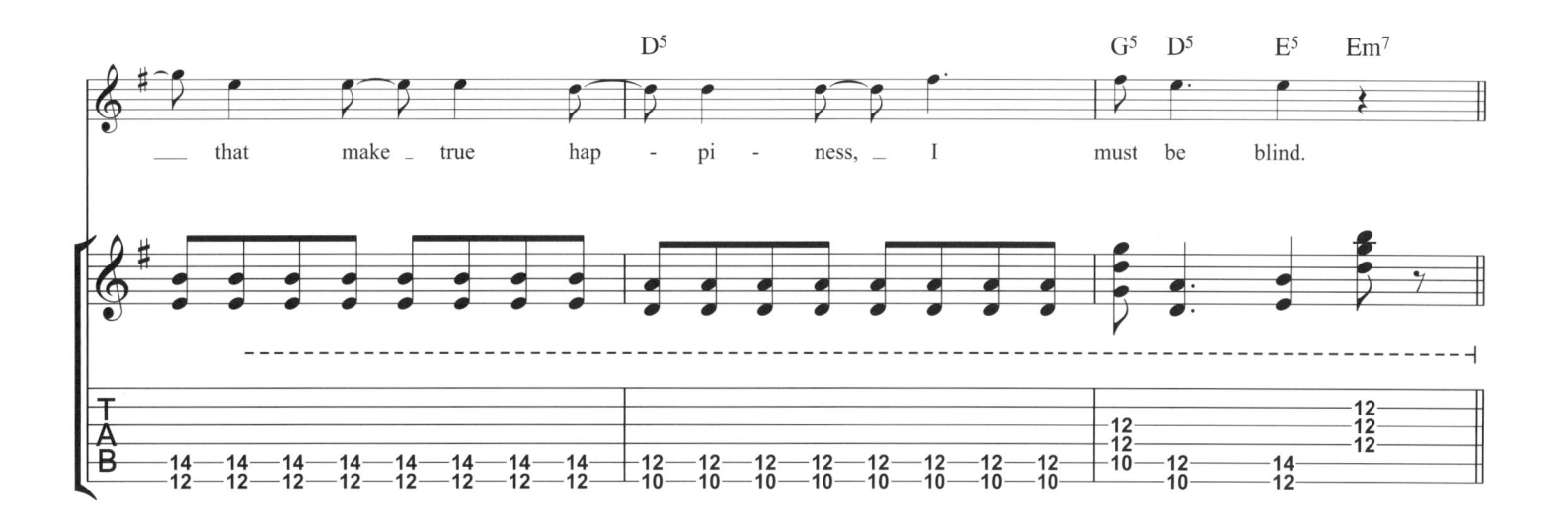

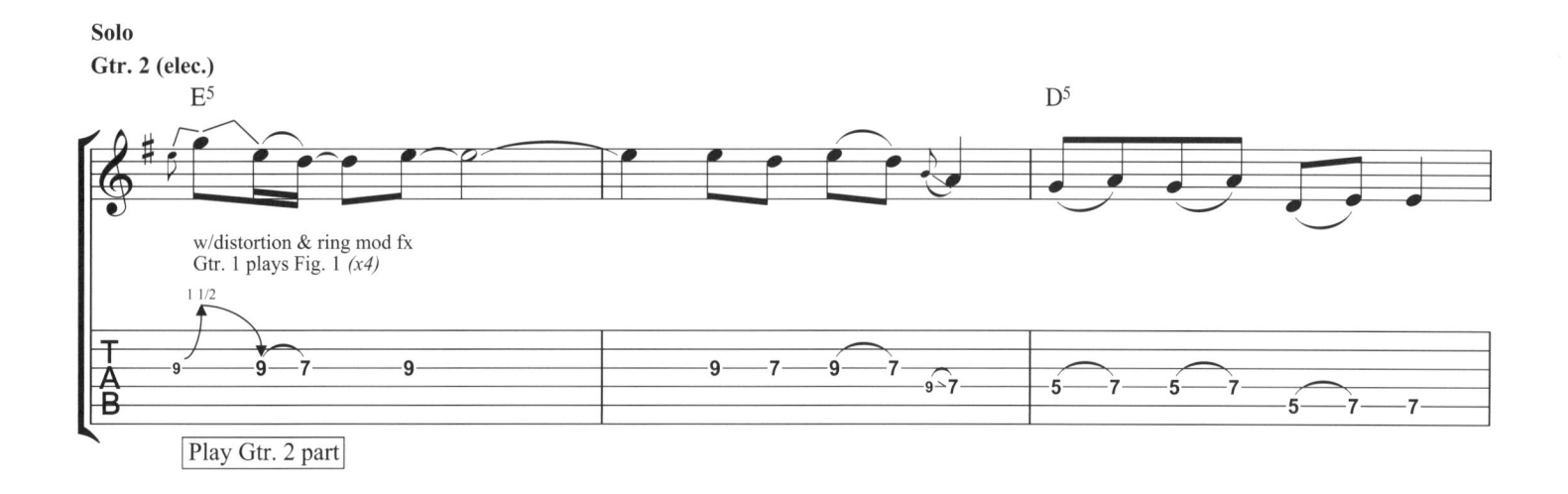

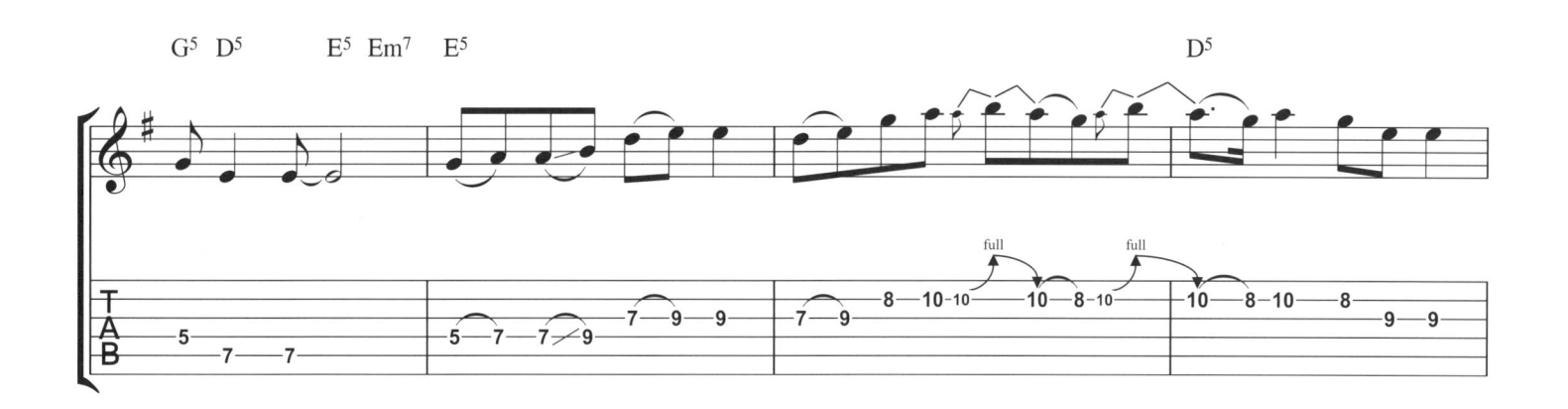

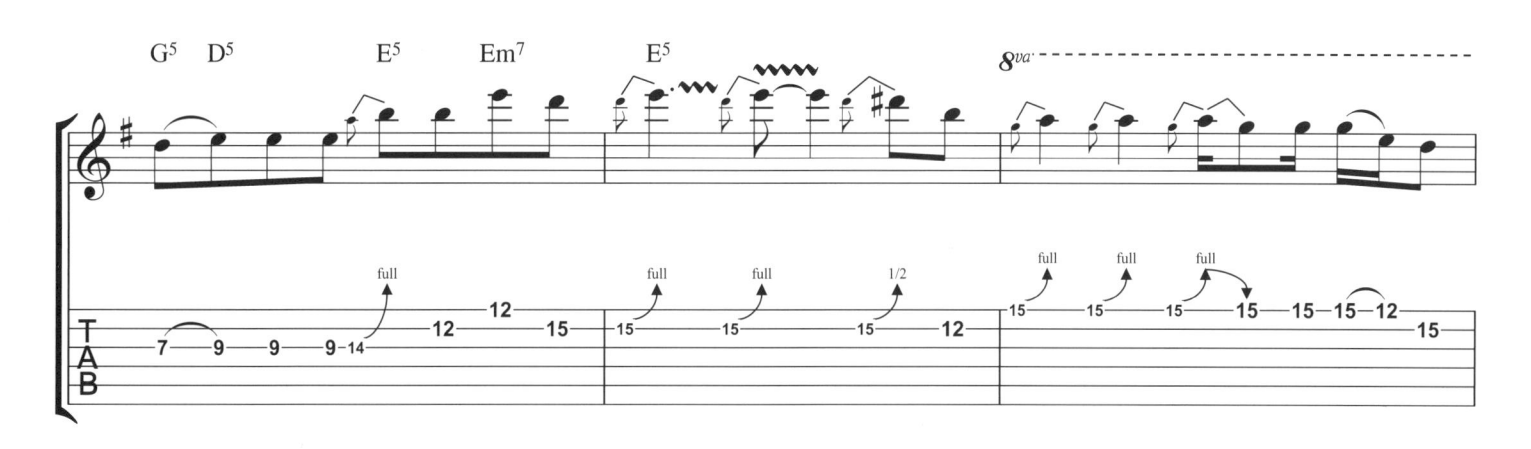

D5
G5 D5 E5 Em7 E5
full
full
D5
G5 D5 E5 Em7
Ring mod off
Gtr. 1 E5
D5
G5 D5 E5 Em7
P.M.
Gtr. 2 tacet
Play Gtr. 1 part
D.S. al Coda
E5
D5
G5 D5 E5 Em7
P.M.

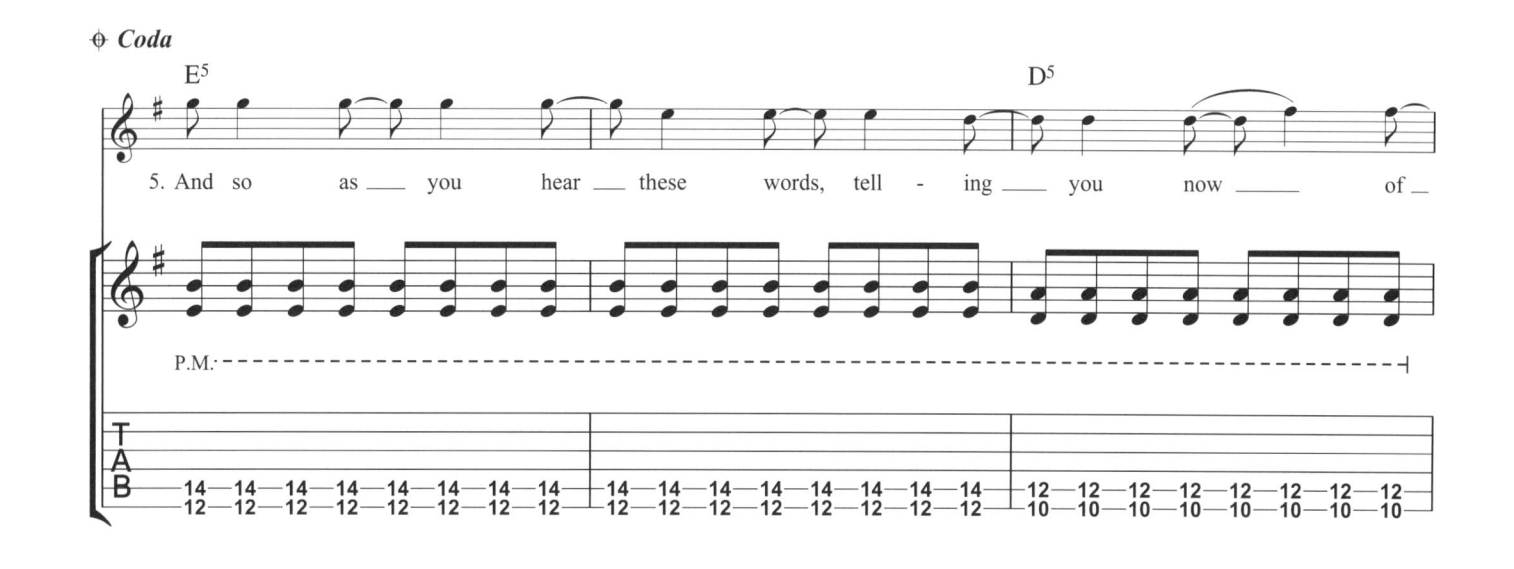

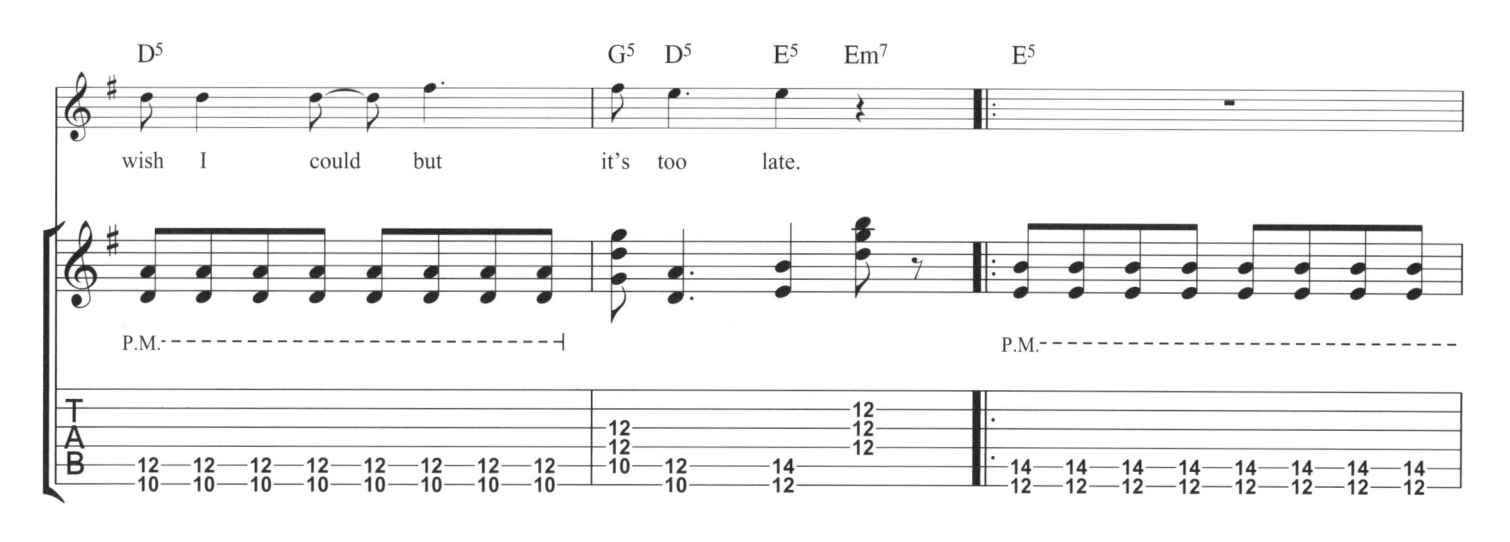

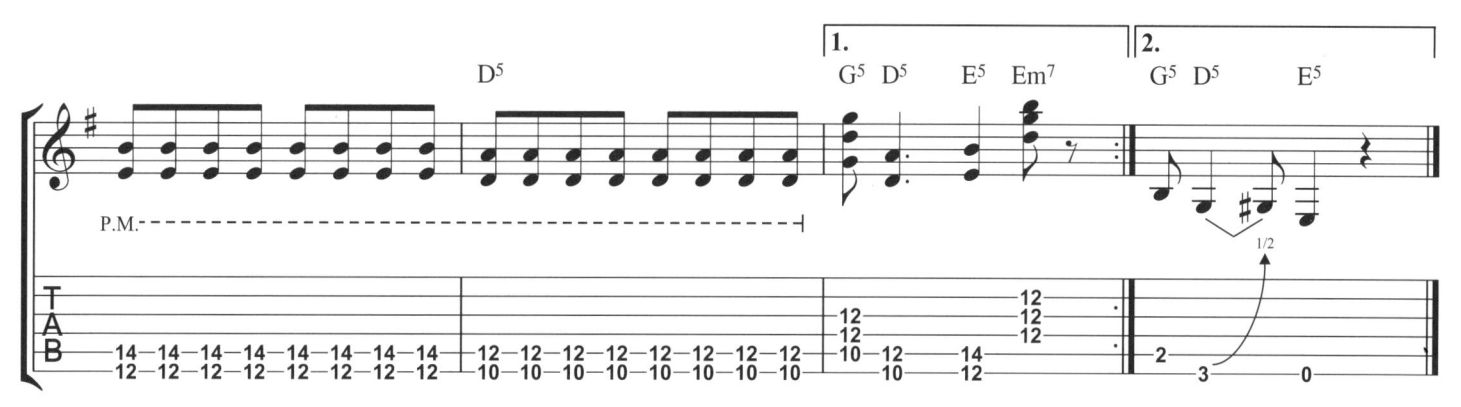

5. And so as you hear these words, telling you now of my state. I tell you to enjoy life I wish I could but it's too late.

pour some sugar on me

**Words and Music by
Steve Clark, Phil Collen, Joe Elliott, Robert John 'Mutt' Lange & Rick Savage**

© Copyright 1987 Bludgeon Riffola Limited/Out Of Pocket Productions Limited.
Universal Music Publishing Limited/Sony/ATV Music Publishing.
All rights in Germany administered by Universal Music Publ. GmbH.
All Rights Reserved. International Copyright Secured.

Full performance demo: track 7
Backing only: track 14

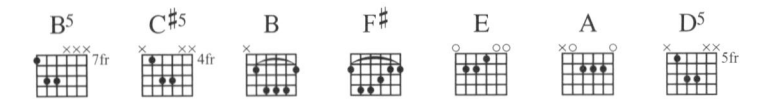

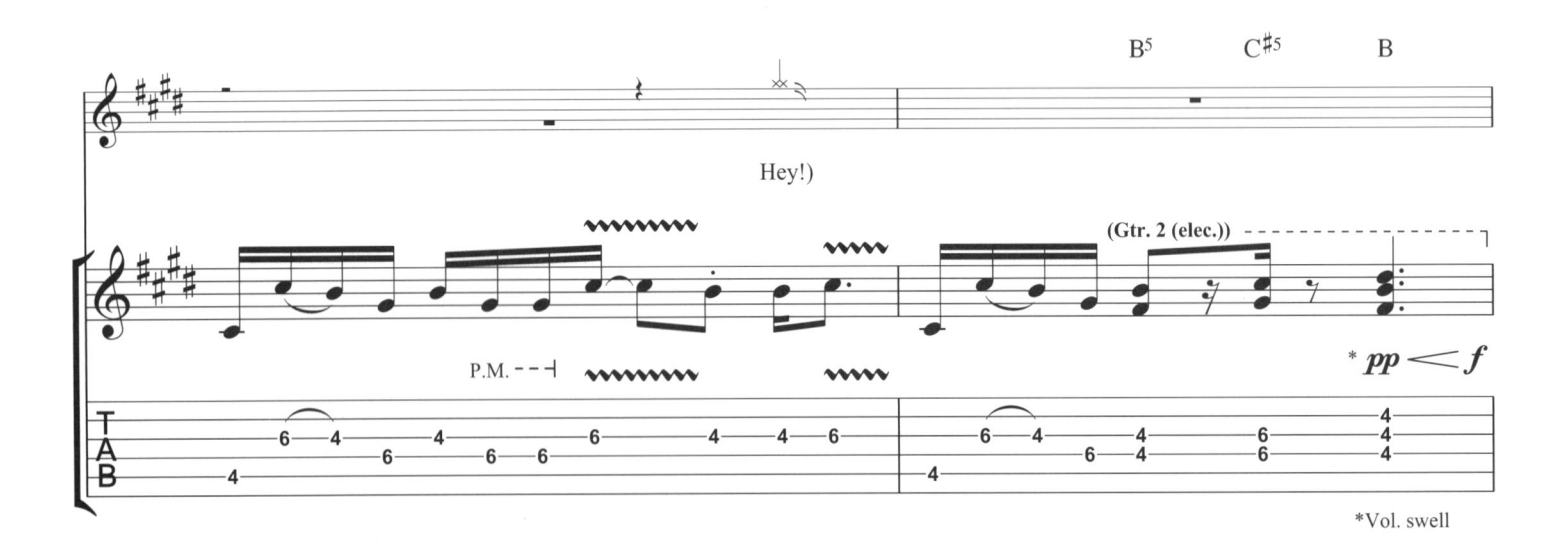

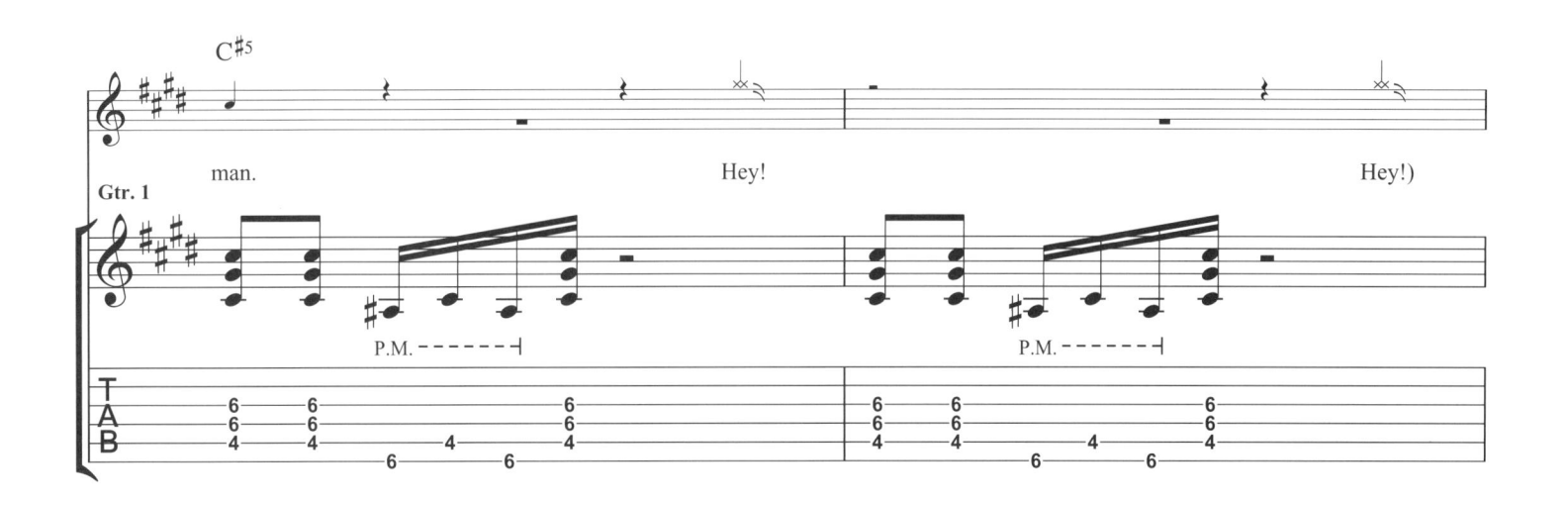

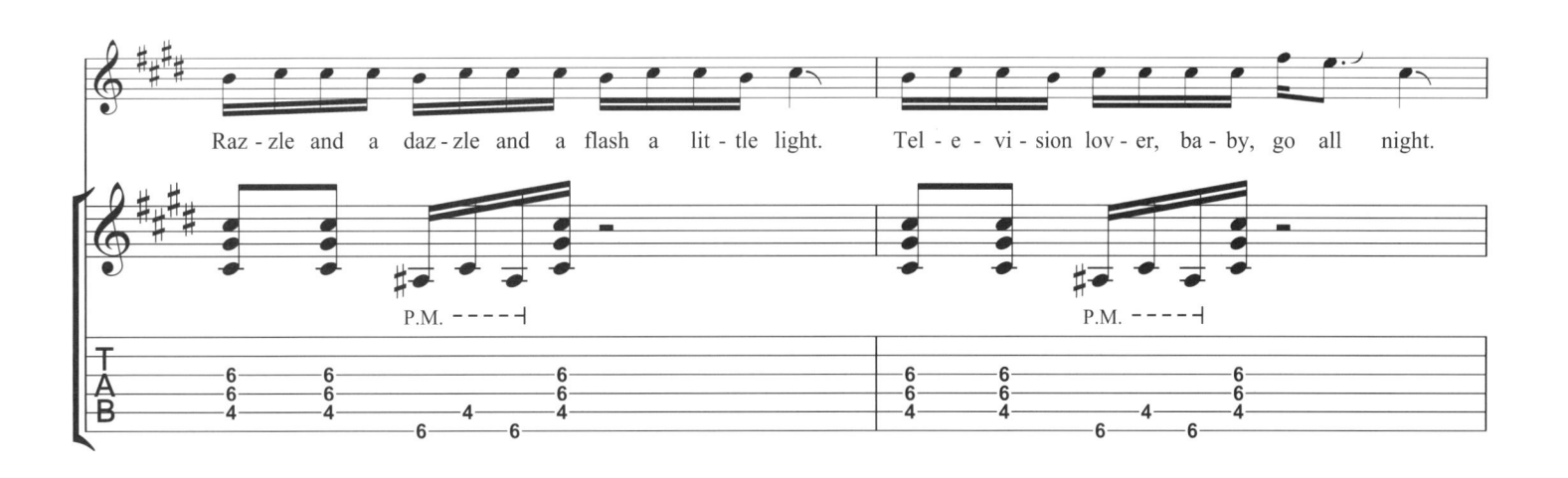

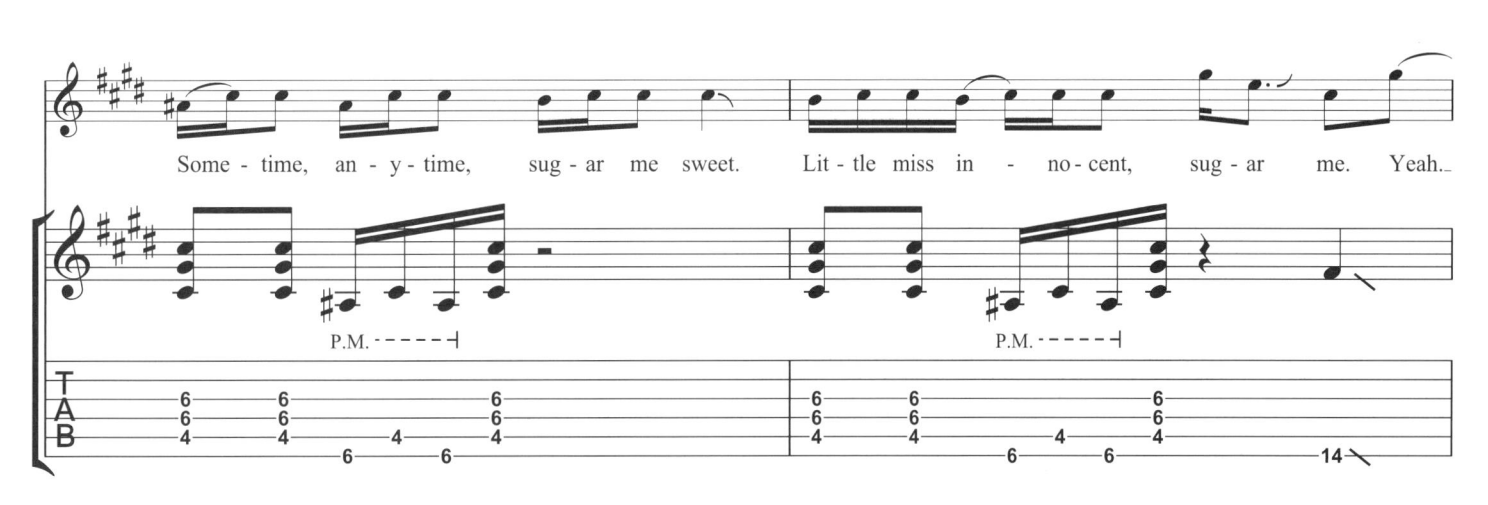

Lookin' like a tramp, like a video vamp. Demolition woman, can I be your man? (Your man. Hey! Hey!)

Razzle and a dazzle and a flash a little light. Television lover, baby, go all night.

Sometime, anytime, sugar me sweet. Little miss innocent, sugar me. Yeah..

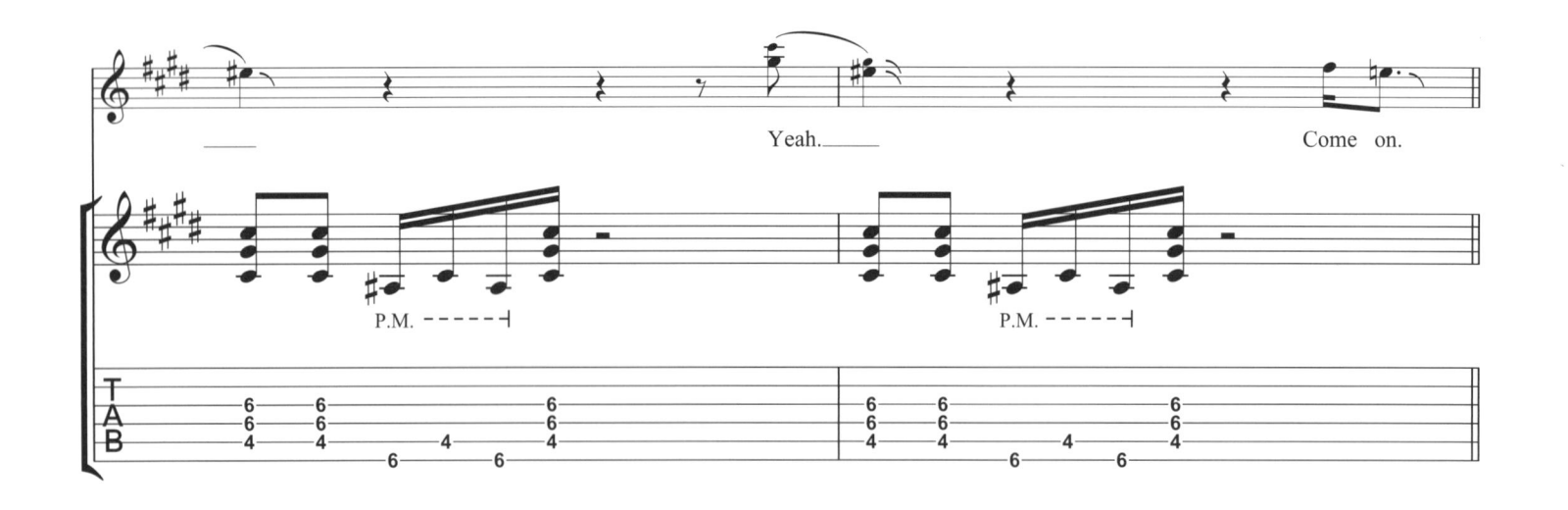

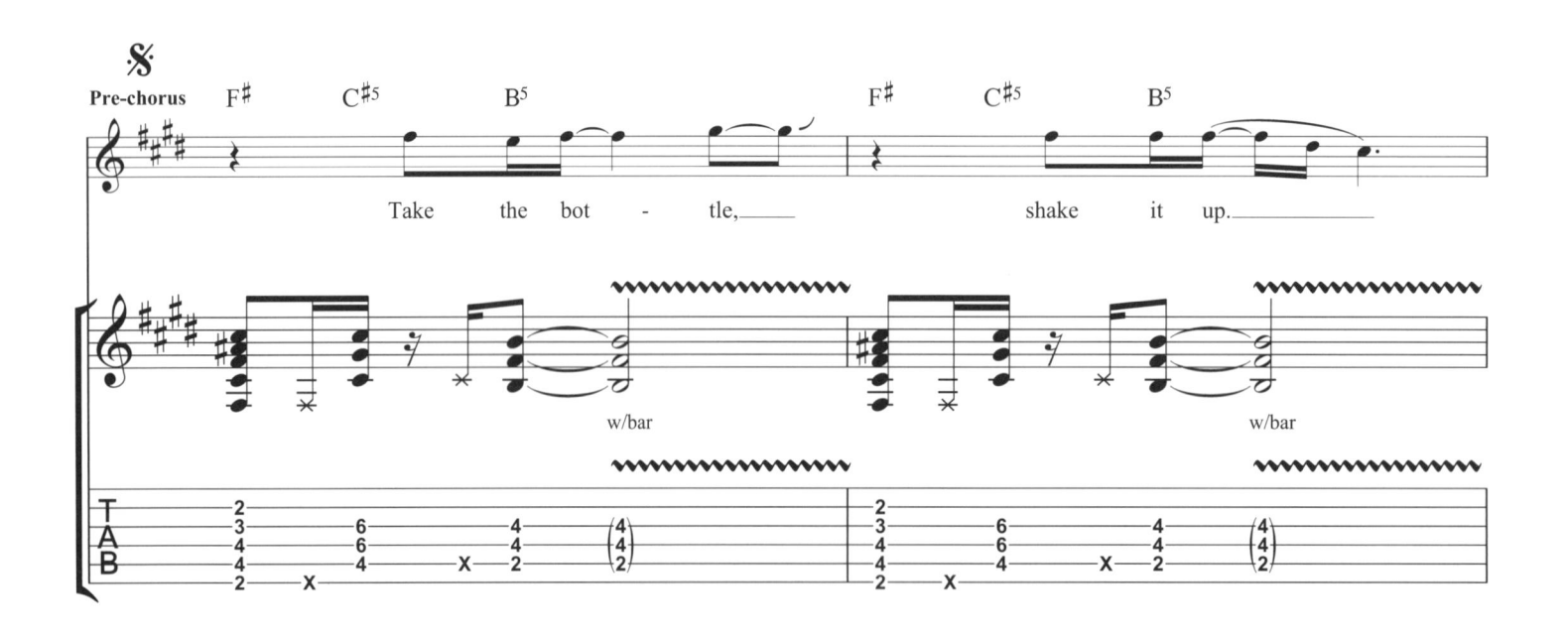

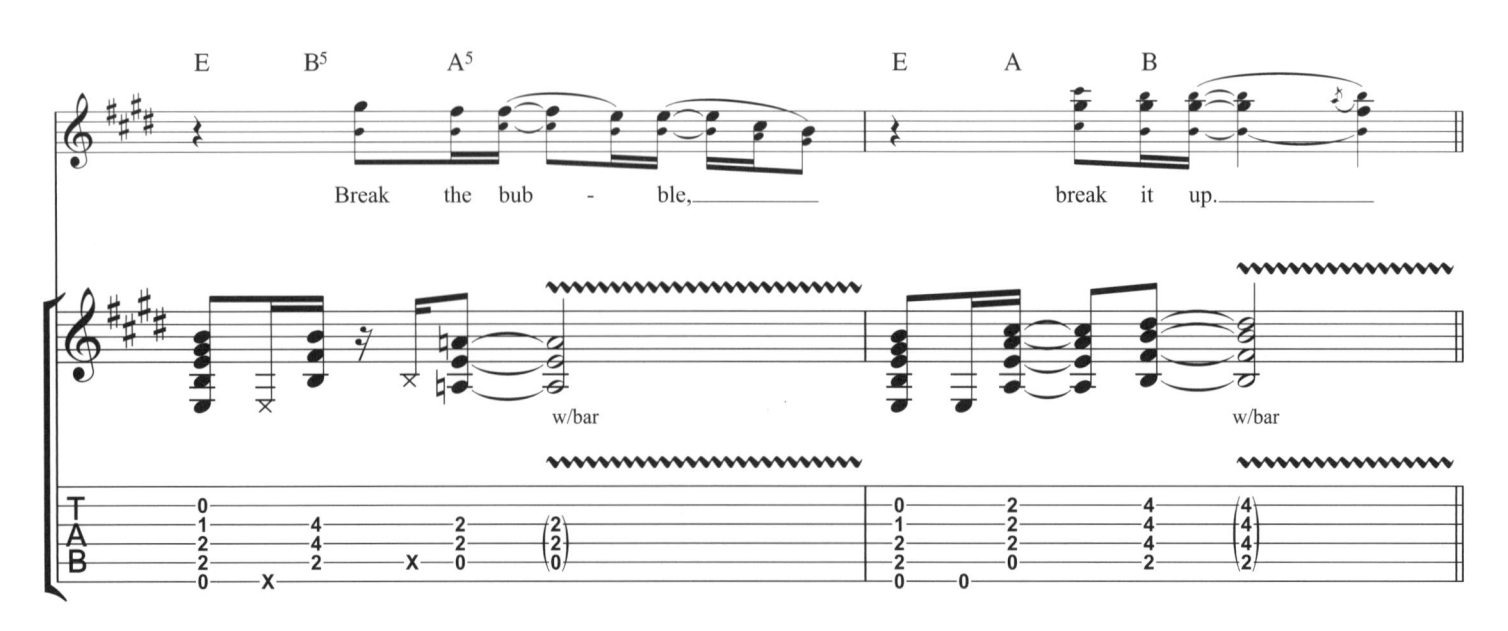

Yeah. Come on.

Pre-chorus

Take the bot - tle, shake it up.

Break the bub - ble, break it up.

55

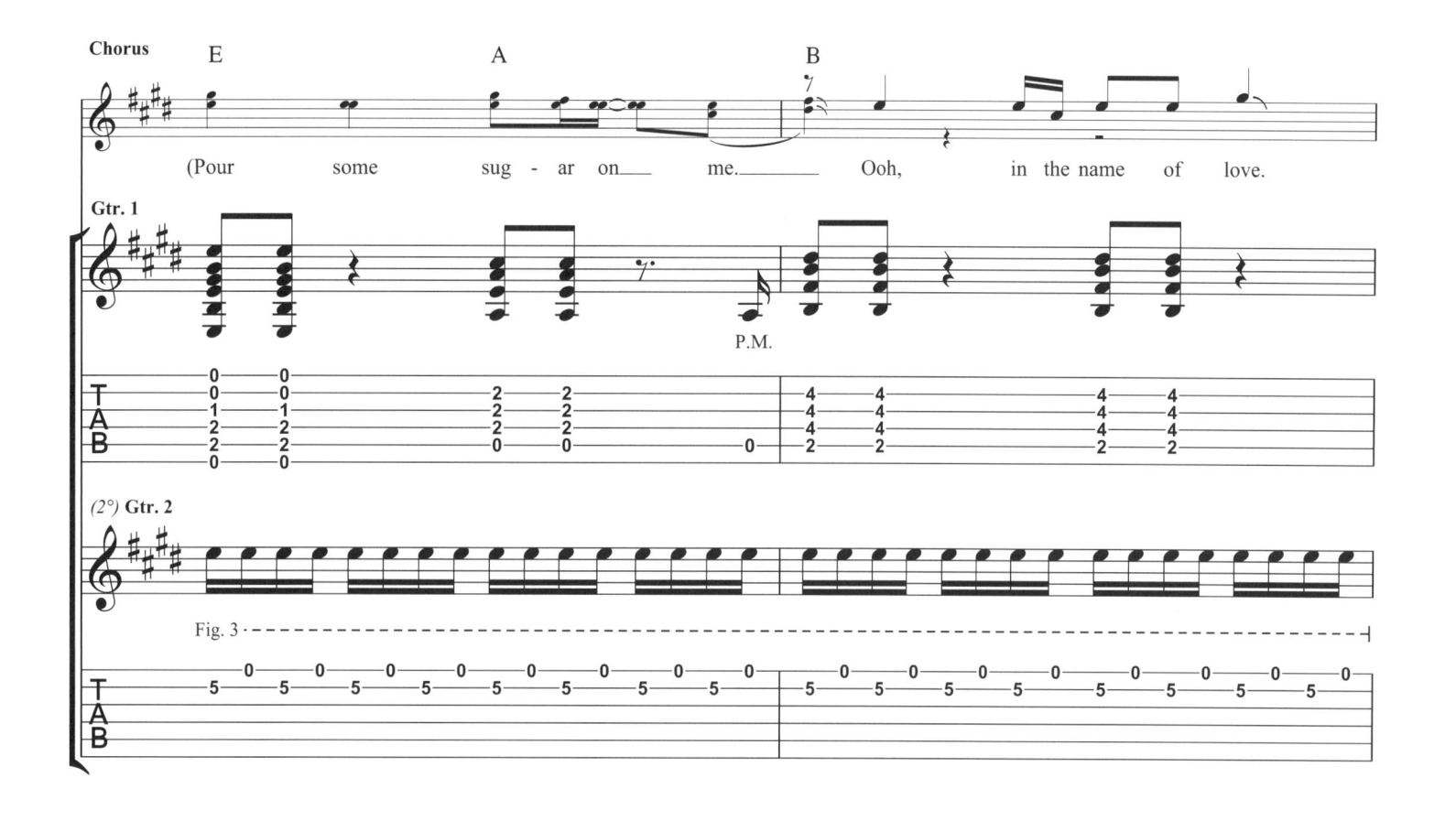

I'm hot, stick-y sweet, from my head to my feet, yeah.

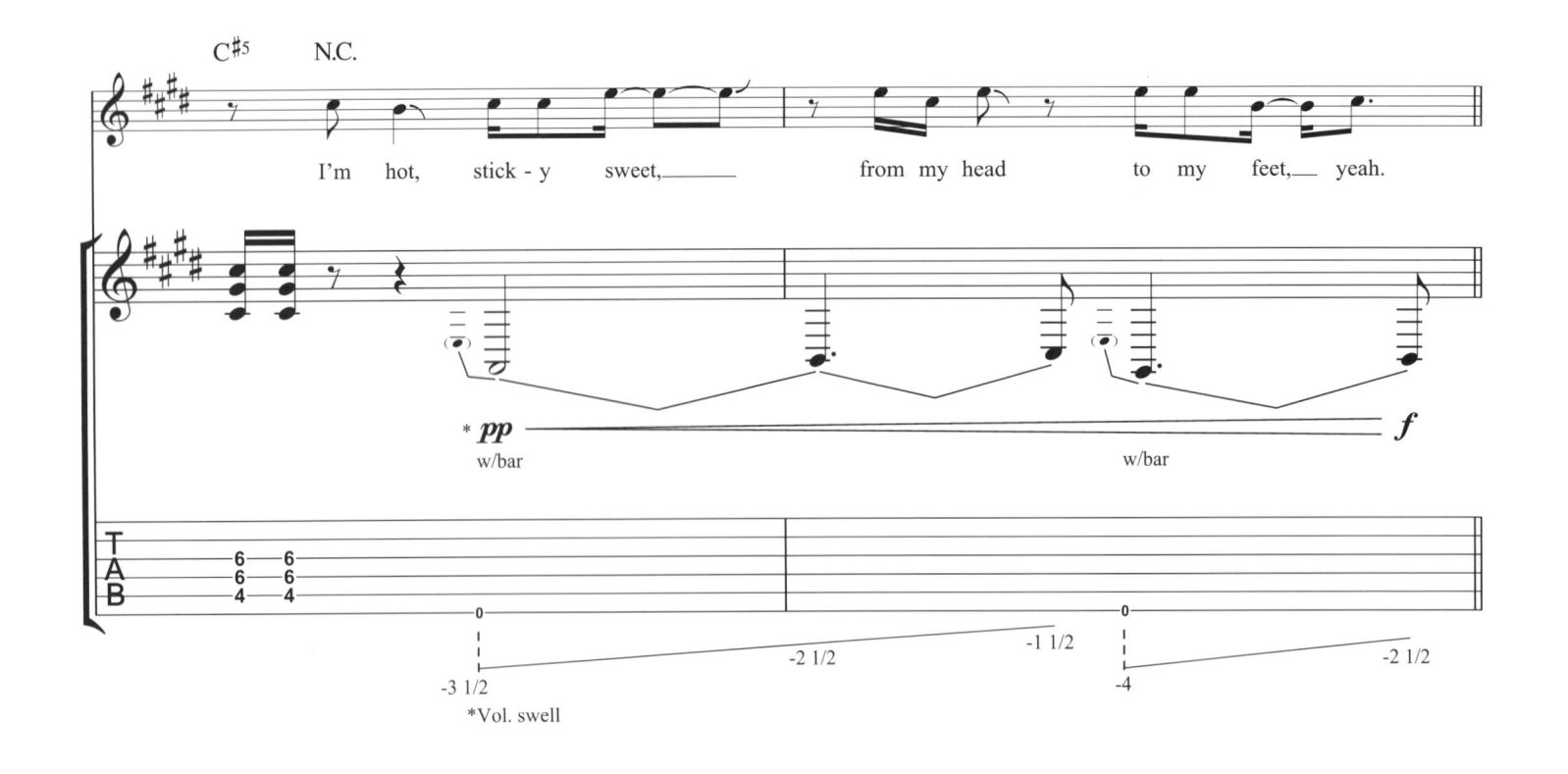

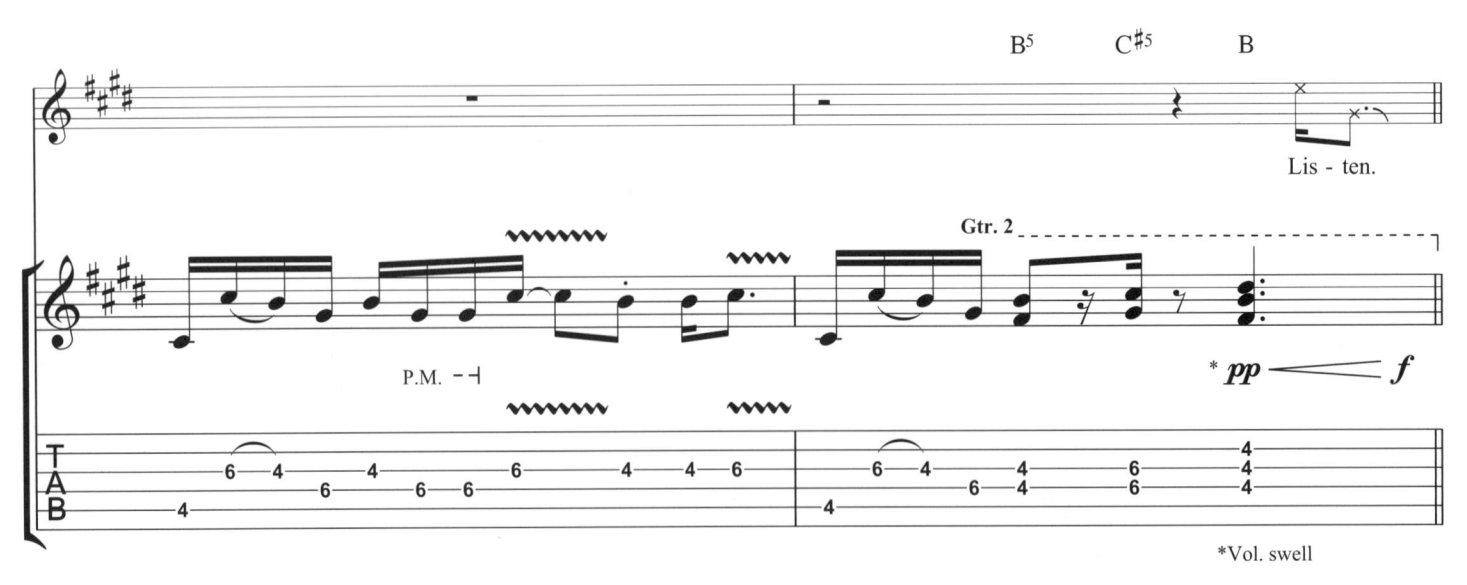

Lis-ten.

Verse
N.C.
2. Red__ light, yel-low light, green a light, go! Cra-zy lit-tle wo-man in a one man show.
Gtr. 2 tacet
Mir-ror queen, man-ne-quin, rhy-thm of a love. Sweet dream, sac-cha-rine, loos-en up. (Loos-en__
w/ bar
-1 1/2
C#5
__ up.) Uh, loos-en up. You got to
P.M.
Fig. 2
Gtr. 2

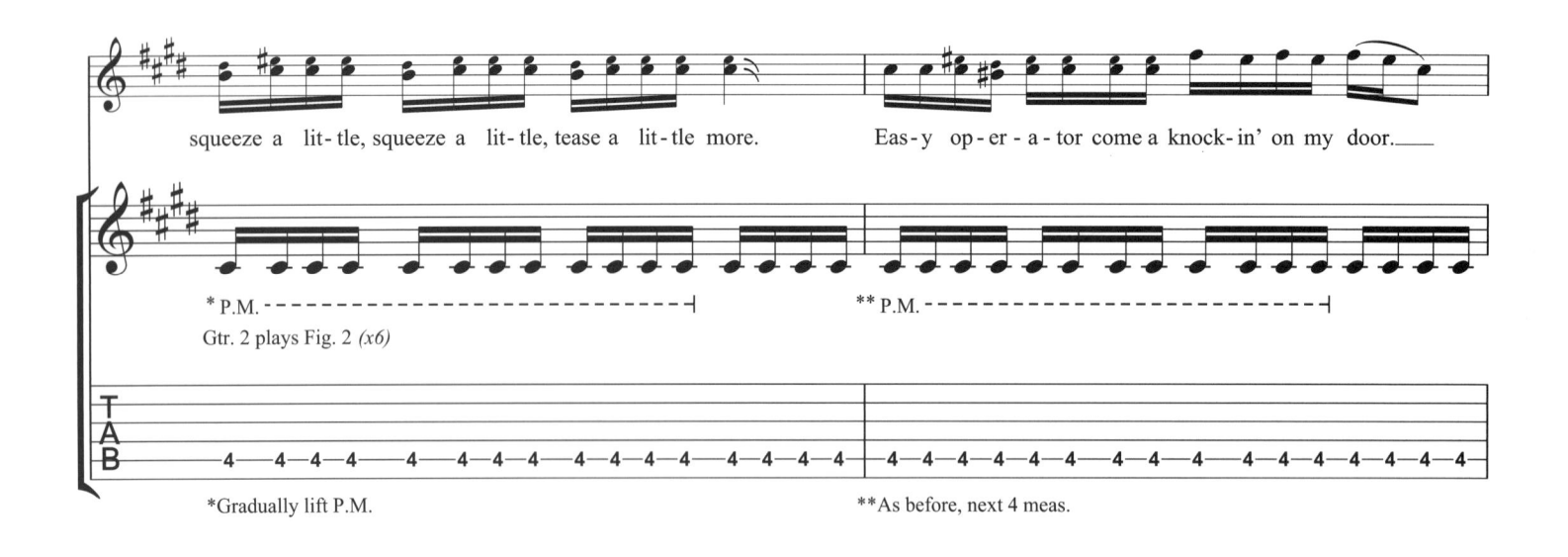

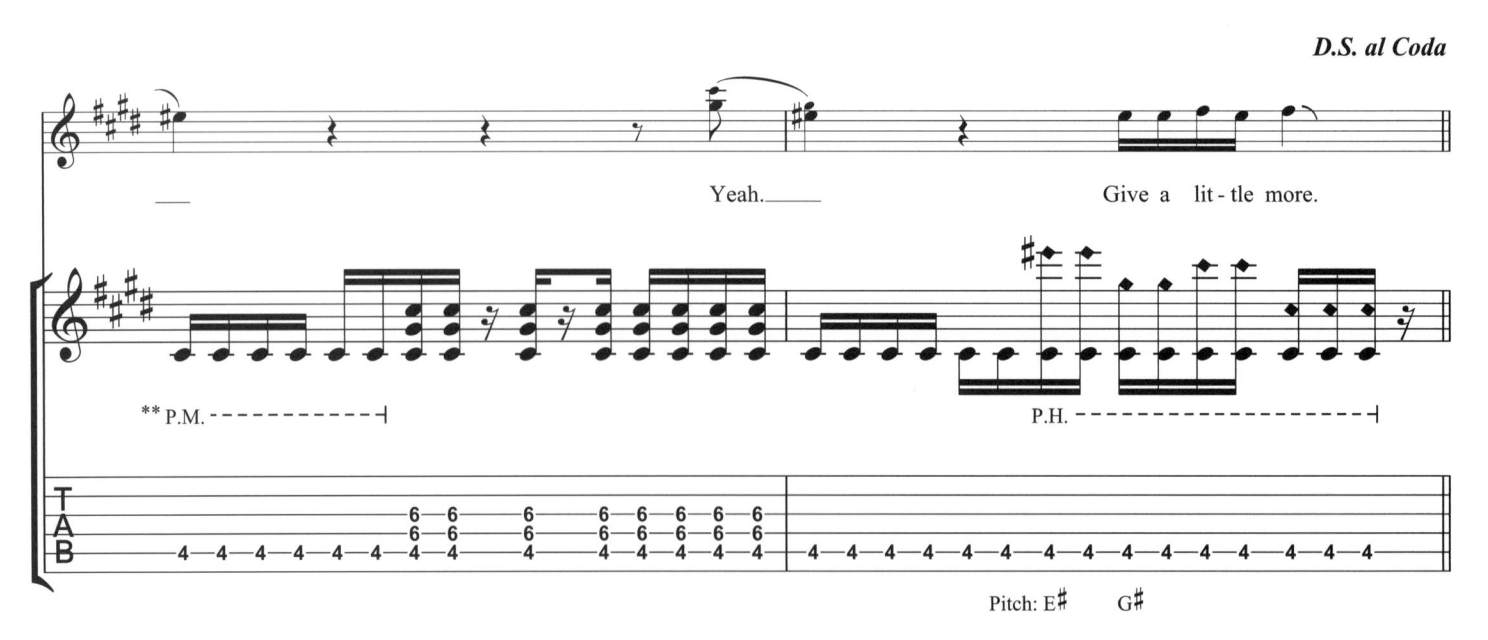

squeeze a lit-tle, squeeze a lit-tle, tease a lit-tle more. Eas-y op-er-a-tor come a knock-in' on my door.

*P.M.
Gtr. 2 plays Fig. 2 (x6)
**P.M.

*Gradually lift P.M.
**As before, next 4 meas.

Some-time, an-y-time, sug-ar me sweet. Lit-tle miss in-no-cent, sug-ar me. Yeah.

**P.M.
**P.M.

D.S. al Coda

Yeah. Give a lit-tle more.

**P.M.
P.H.

Pitch: E# G#

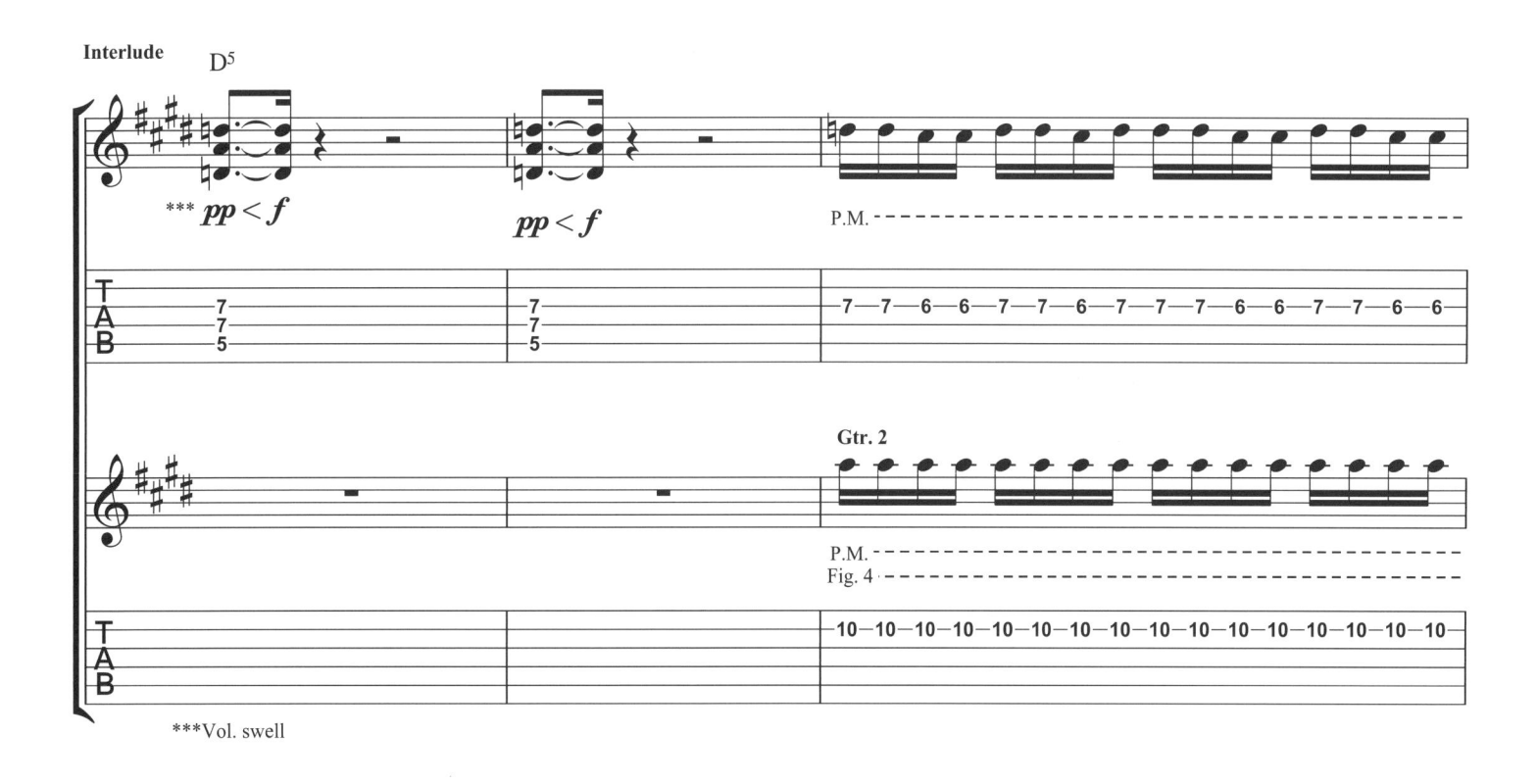

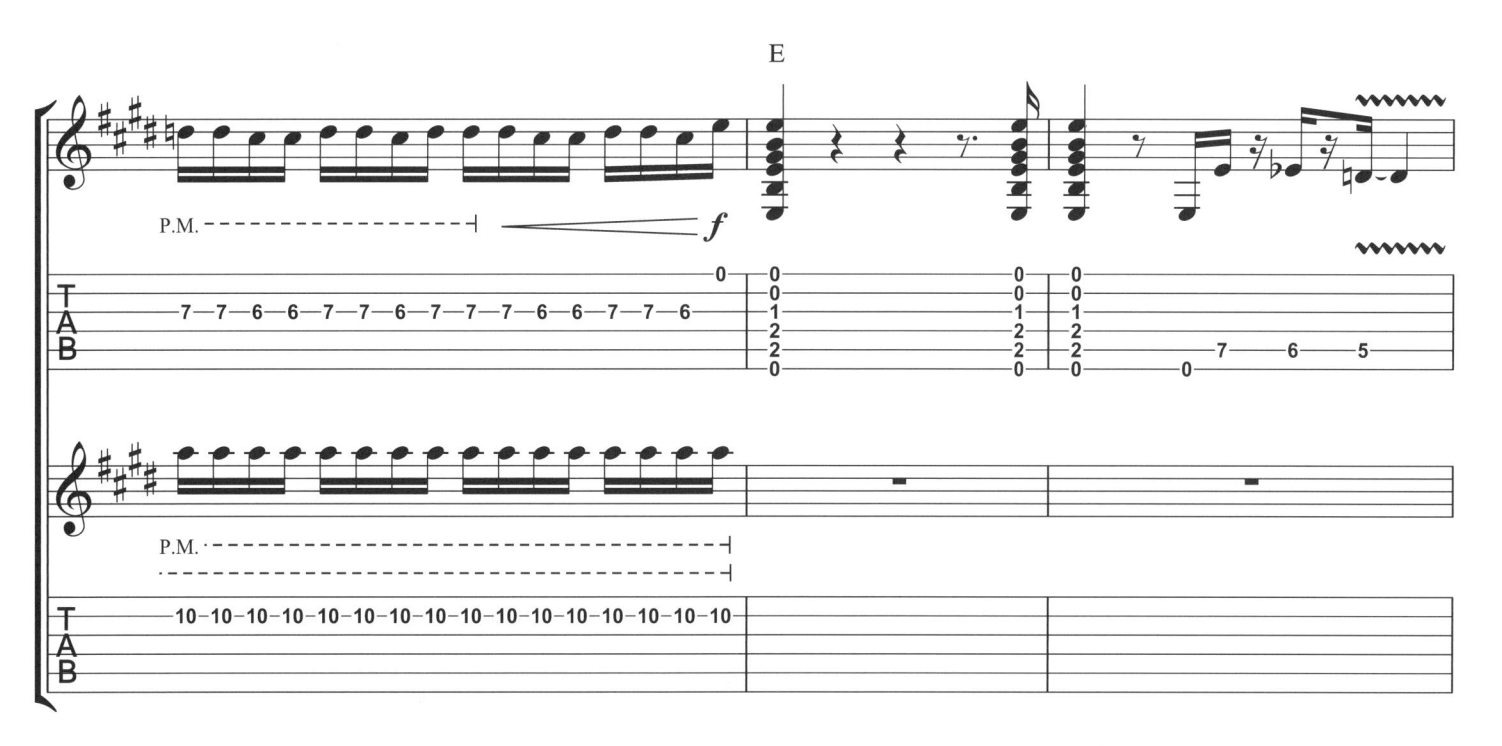

Coda

I'm hot, stick-y sweet, from my head to my feet, yeah.

Interlude

***Vol. swell

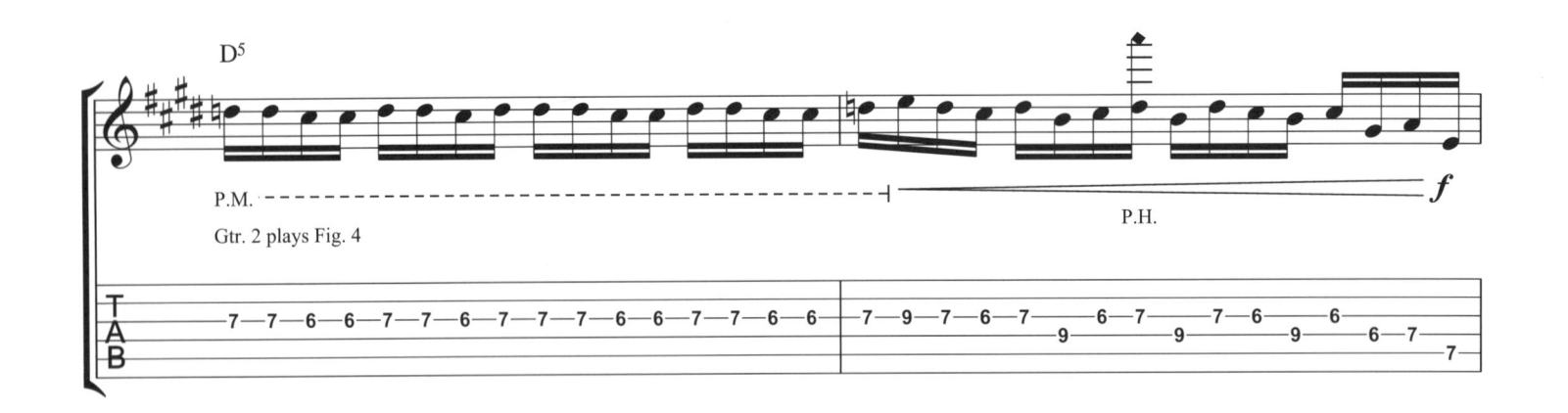

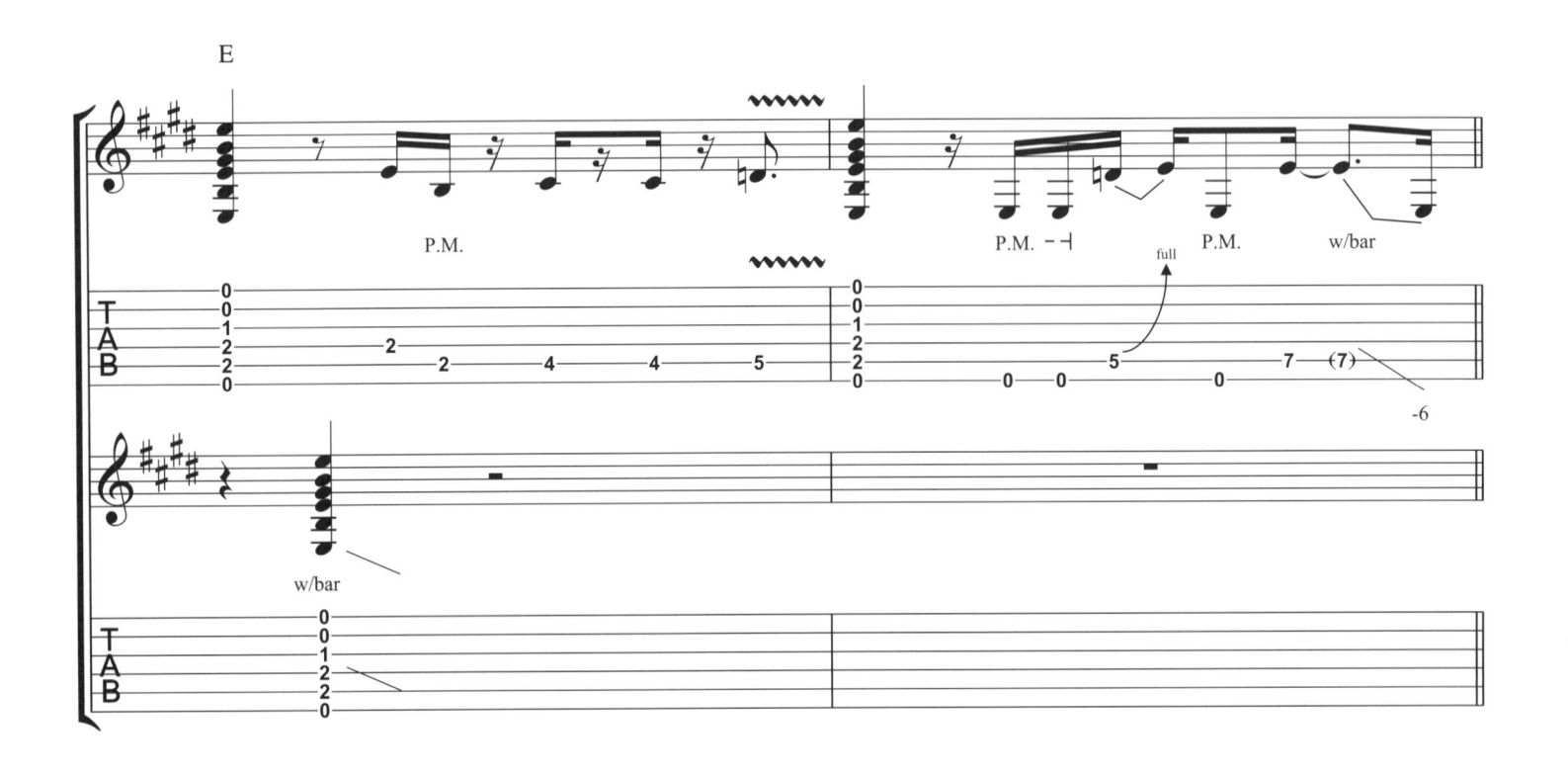

(You got the peach - es, I got the cream. Sweet to taste. Sac - cha - rin. 'Cause I'm

hot, so hot, stick - y sweet from my head, my head a - to my feet.
Hot, hot, sweet. Head, head, my feet.)

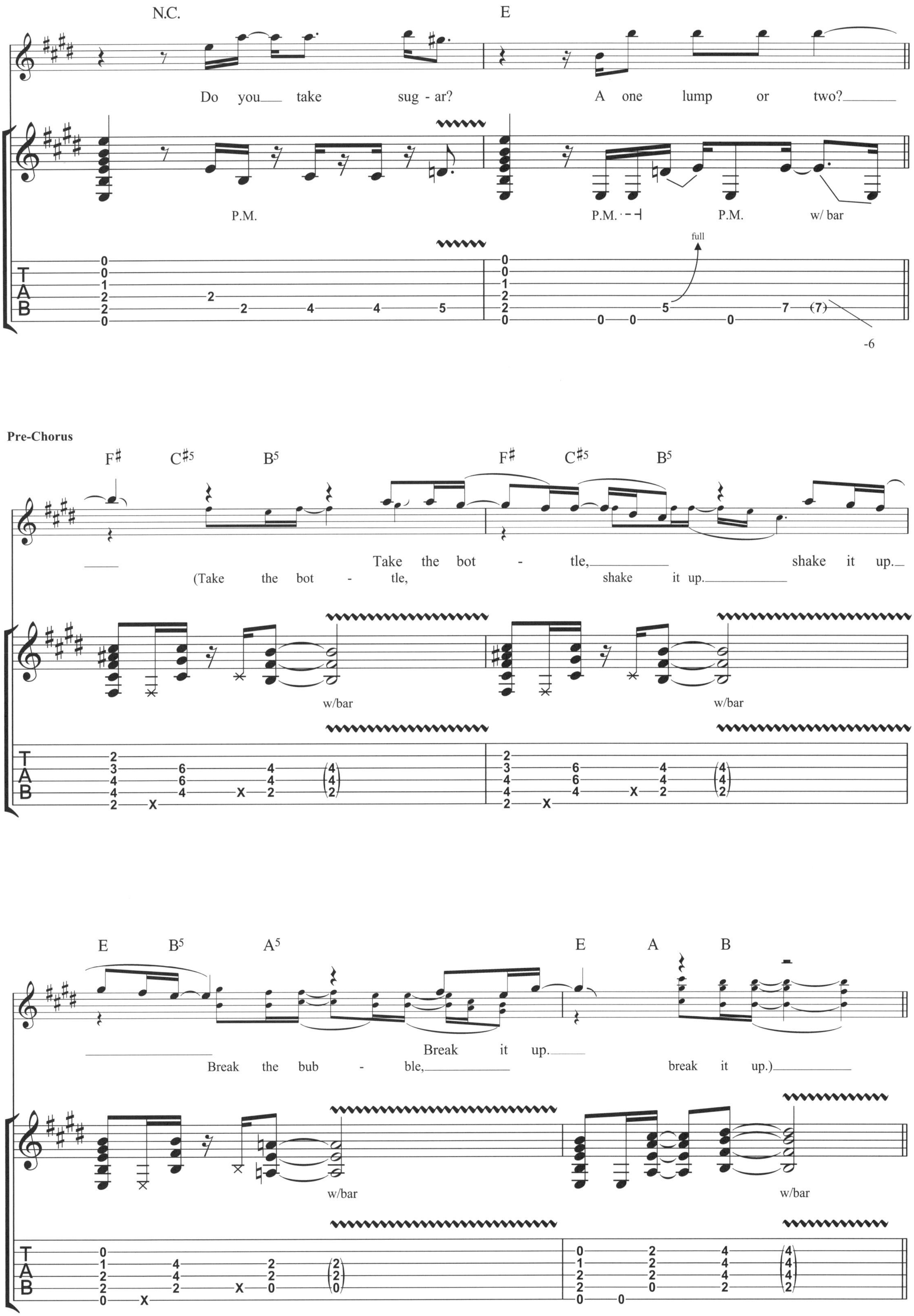
N.C.
E
Do you take sug - ar?
A one lump or two?
P.M.
P.M.
P.M.
w/ bar
full
Pre-Chorus
F♯ C♯5 B5 F♯ C♯5 B5
Take the bot - tle, shake it up.
(Take the bot - tle, shake it up.
w/bar
w/bar
E B5 A5 E A B
Break it up.
Break the bub - ble, break it up.)
w/bar
w/bar

Chorus

(Pour some sugar on me. Ooh, in the name of love.

Gtr. 2 plays Fig. 1 (x7)

Pour some sugar on me. Come on, fire me up.

Pour your sugar on me. I can't get enough.

Gtr. 3 (elec.) plays ad lib. sim.

Pour some sugar on me. Oh, in the name of love.

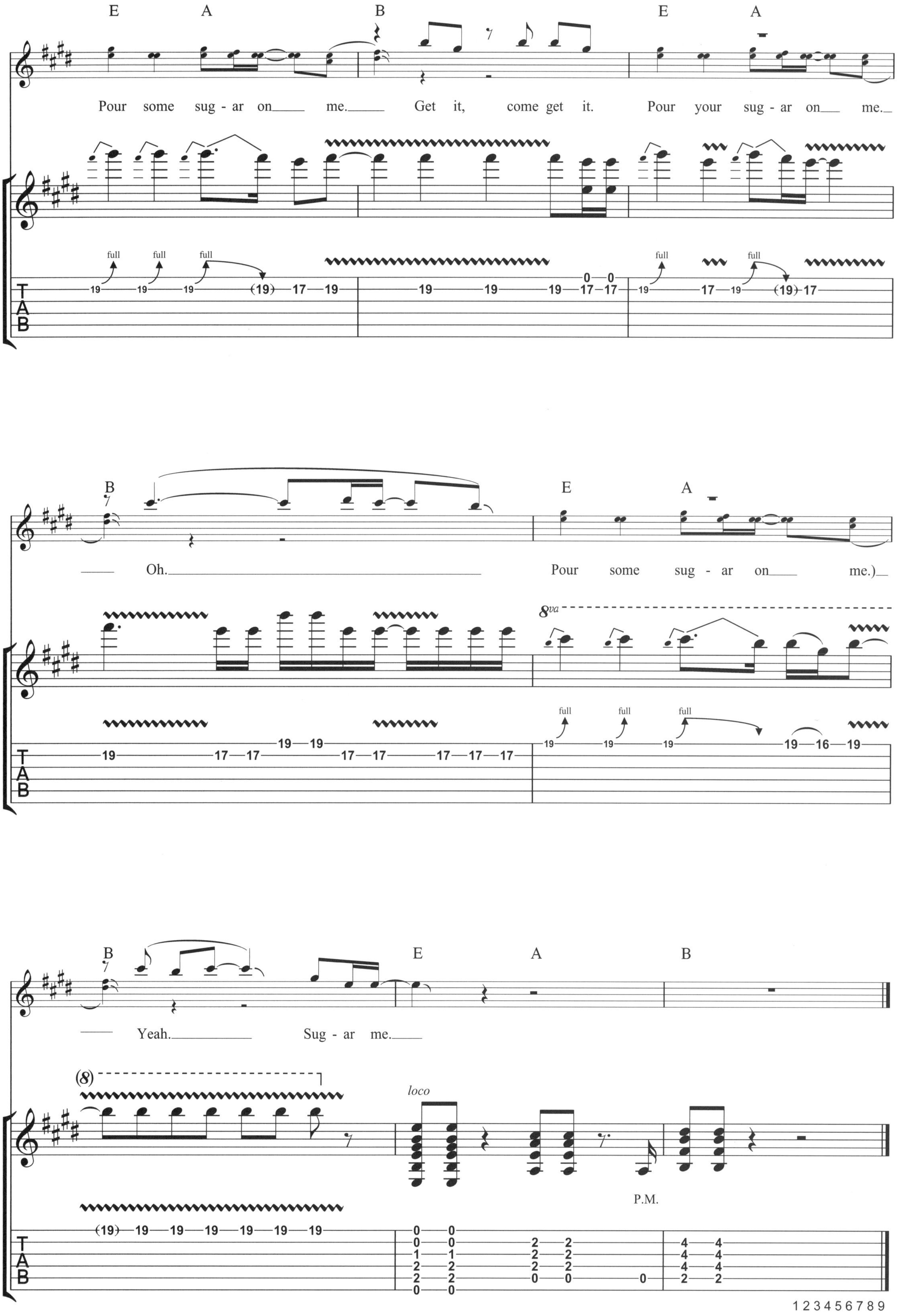
E A B E A
Pour some sug - ar on me. Get it, come get it. Pour your sug - ar on me.
full full full full full
B E A
Oh. Pour some sug - ar on me.)
8va
full full full
B E A B
Yeah. Sug - ar me.
(8)
loco
P.M.
TAB

1 2 3 4 5 6 7 8 9

CD track listing

Full instrumental performances (with guitar)...

1. **ace of spades**
   (Clarke/Kilmister/Taylor) Motor Music Ltd.
2. **the boys are back in town**
   (Lynott) Universal Music Publishing Limited.
3. **breaking the law**
   (Downing/Halford/Tipton)
   EMI Music Publishing Ltd./EMI Songs Ltd.
4. **the number of the beast**
   (Harris) Imagem London Limited.
5. **smoke on the water**
   (Blackmore/Gillan/Glover/Lord/Paice) HEC Music.
6. **paranoid**
   (Butler/Iommi/Osbourne/Ward) Westminster Music Ltd.
7. **pour some sugar on me**
   (Allen/Clark/Collen/Elliott/Lange/Savage)
   Universal Music Publishing Limited/
   Sony/ATV Music Publishing (UK) Limited.

Backing tracks (without guitar)...

8. **ace of spades**
9. **the boys are back in town**
10. **breaking the law**
11. **the number of the beast**
12. **smoke on the water**
13. **paranoid**
14. **pour some sugar on me**

To remove your CD from the plastic sleeve, lift the small lip to break the perforation. Replace the disc after use for convenient storage.